P9-DND-791

LAST UNSPOILED PLACE

UTAH'S LOGAN CANYON

There were times when we were down
emotionally or mentally and we found ourselves
refreshed after a walk in the canyon. It was our
canyon, though we knew we shared it with
every lover of nature.
—Mary Ellsworth,
recalling a lifetime of visits to Logan Canyon

LAST UNSPOILED PLACE

UTAH'S LOGAN CANYON

BY MICHAEL S. SWEENEY

NATIONAL GEOGRAPHIC
WASHINGTON, D.C.

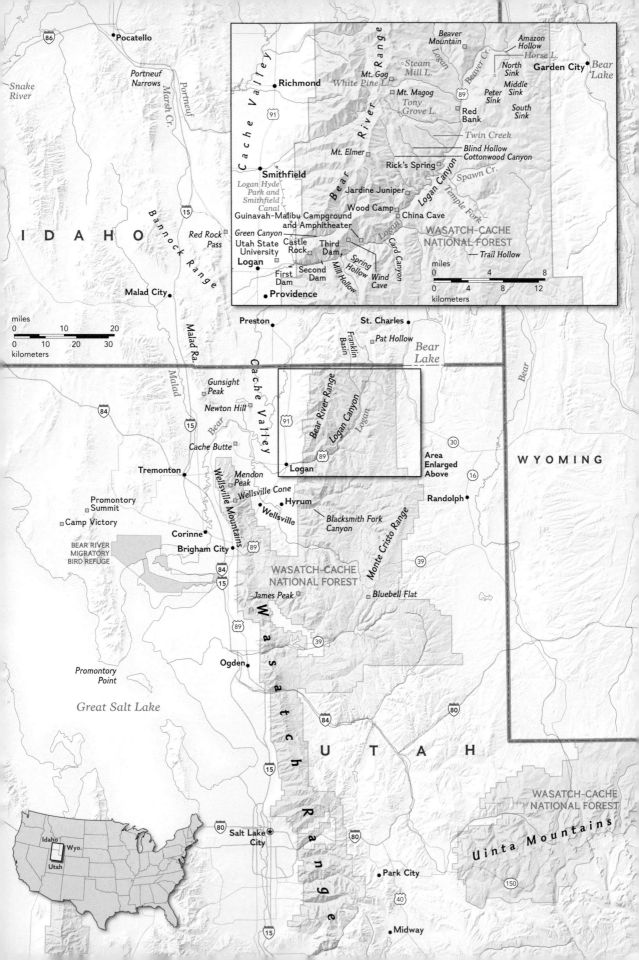

Inset map (upper right):

Beaver Mountain

Steam Mill L.

Amazon Hollow

Horse L.

North Sink

Logan

Beaver Cr.

Mt. Gog

White Pine L.

Garden City

Bear Lake

Richmond

Cache Valley

Bear River Range

Mt. Magog

Tony Grove L.

Peter Sink

Middle Sink

South Sink

Red Bank

Smithfield

Twin Creek

Mt. Elmer

Rick's Spring

Blind Hollow

Cottonwood Canyon

Spawn Cr.

Logan Hyde Park and Smithfield Canal

Jardine Juniper

Logan Canyon

Temple Fork

Guinavah-Malibu Campground and Amphitheater

Wood Camp

China Cave

Green Canyon

Logan

WASATCH-CACHE NATIONAL FOREST

Utah State University

Castle Rock

Third Dam

Spring Hollow

Card Canyon

Trail Hollow

Logan

First Dam

Second Dam

Mill Hollow

Wind Cave

Providence

miles 0 4 8
kilometers 0 4 8 12

Main map:

86

Pocatello

Snake River

Portneuf Narrows

Portneuf

Marsh Cr.

Richmond

Cache Valley

Bear River Range

Steam Mill L.

White Pine L.

15

I D A H O

Red Rock Pass

Bannock Range

Smithfield

Logan Hyde Park and Smithfield Canal

Malad City

Malad Ra.

Malad

Preston

St. Charles

Pat Hollow

Bear Lake

Franklin Basin

miles 0 10 20
kilometers 0 10 20 30

84

15

Bear

Gunsight Peak

Newton Hill

Cache Valley

91

Bear River Range

Logan Canyon

Logan

Bear Lake

30

W Y O M I N G

Cache Butte

Area Enlarged Above

89

16

Tremonton

Mendon Peak

Wellsville Cone

Hyrum

Randolph

Promontory Summit

Wellsville Mountains

Wellsville

Blacksmith Fork Canyon

Camp Victory

Corinne

Brigham City

89

BEAR RIVER MIGRATORY BIRD REFUGE

84

15

WASATCH-CACHE NATIONAL FOREST

James Peak

Monte Cristo Range

Bluebell Flat

39

89

W a s a t c h

39

Ogden

Promontory Point

Great Salt Lake

U T A H

84

80

WASATCH-CACHE NATIONAL FOREST

Idaho

Wyo.

Utah

R a n g e

80

Salt Lake City

80

Uinta Mountains

15

Park City

150

40

Midway

15

CONTENTS

PAGE 1: *John Decker hangs from a rock wall in Logan Canyon, a premier destination for sport climbers.*
PRECEDING PAGES: *A stream burbles out of Spring Hollow on its way to meet the Logan River.*

BONNEVILLE SHORELINE TO SPRING HOLLOW

BONNEVILLE SHORELINE TO SPRING HOLLOW

Frank Clark didn't set out to become a legend when he killed Utah's last grizzly bear. It was strictly business.

Clark was a practical man. Born in 1879 in southern Idaho, he briefly attended school before heading for a job under the open sky. Beginning in 1911, he herded sheep each summer in the canyons and forests of northern Utah. He slept in a tent and watched his flocks graze in the fir- and juniper-covered crags of Logan Canyon. His spotted dog, Jenny, kept him constant company.

Grizzly and brown bears "infested" Logan Canyon, he said. Normally they stuffed themselves with roots, berries, and the occasional fish or rodent, but Clark's meandering mutton provided an irresistible, movable feast—a veritable bear buffet. Clark's losses angered him.

"I have sworn eternal vengeance on bears and it shall be mine," Clark said. Bears stole and ate 150 of his sheep in one summer alone. He fought back with traps and bullets, satisfied that in only two of his forty-five backcountry summers did he fail to kill at least one bear. He pronounced bear steak to be "good meat."

A giant grizzly continually troubled him but proved elusive. Old Three Toes, the locals called him, and sometimes Old Ephraim. The latter, biblical name resonated with Utah's Mormons, who associated it with patriarchal authority and considered it fitting for the king of carnivores. Clark identified the grizzly by its deformed paw prints in the appropriately named Bear River mountains of Logan Canyon.

Between 1913 and 1923, Old Ephraim quietly and cunningly struck every summer at Clark's sheep. He "never seemed to pick on the same herd twice in succession," Clark said, "but roamed around for several miles in the proximity of the spring where he bathed and would take only one or two sheep from each separate camp." One year Clark made Old Ephraim drop a sheep with the crack of a rifle shot, but Clark didn't injure the bear.

THE SKULL OF OLD EPHRAIM, THE LAST OF THE CANYON'S GRIZZLY BEARS, OCCUPIES A PLACE OF HONOR IN THE UTAH STATE UNIVERSITY LIBRARY.

PRECEDING PAGES: THE MOUNTAINS THAT FLANK LOGAN CANYON RISE IN MUTED WINTER COLORS ABOVE THE WILLOWS AND PLOWED FIELDS OF SOUTHERN CACHE VALLEY.

BRYAN LUNDAHL, AN OUT-
FITTER AND GUIDE, HEADS
TOWARD WHITE PINE
LAKE WITH SON TYSON, IN
COWBOY HAT, DAUGHTER
ANDREA, AND SON LANCE.

Clark set trap after trap in the grizzly's wallow, where the bear bathed in water and mud. Each time, Old Ephraim lifted the trap and gently dropped it nearby. Clark lamented that the bear was too smart, winning every time in their "everlasting battle."

In Clark's account, in the late summer of 1923, Old Ephraim carved a fresh wallow in a creek at Trail Hollow, about a dozen miles from the mouth of Logan Canyon. Clark stumbled upon the bear's new bathtub, unoccupied. He put a trap at the bottom and covered it with mud. Satisfied with his work, he walked downstream to camp for the night. He awoke to a star-studded sky and "the most unearthly sound I have ever heard." Grabbing his rifle, he ran out without dressing into a night "darker than hell and too cold for BVDs."

"There came rushing out of the creek bottom the giant form of Old Ephraim walking on his hind feet," Clark recalled. The grizzly carried a steel trap clamped on a foot and about 15 feet of the trap's log chain wrapped around a leg.

"I listened and could hear the chain rattle and so did my teeth," Clark said.

As Old Ephraim approached, Clark opened fire with a small-caliber rifle, hitting the bear repeatedly with steel-ball cartridges. The grizzly staggered and fell dead. Clark hurried three miles to find the closest human at another sheep camp. They skinned Old

Ephraim and burned and buried the carcass. Clark discovered the bear had snapped off aspen trees six inches in diameter as it lurched from the wallow in its agony.

A Boy Scout troop following Clark's directions hiked into the canyon and found Ephraim's grave. The bear appeared to weigh about 1,100 pounds and stood nine feet eleven inches tall. The scouts took the skull, "stinking like mad," according to the scoutmaster's son, and carried it out of the canyon at the end of a pole. The scoutmaster sent the skull to the Smithsonian Institution for its collection as well as confirmation that it belonged to a grizzly. The Smithsonian returned $25 and the news that Old Ephraim was, indeed, *Ursus horribilis*. Since that day, no other grizzlies have been documented in Utah.

In 1978, the Smithsonian agreed to send the skull home on long-term loan. U.S. Senator Orrin Hatch carried the skull in a wooden box on his lap during the trip's last leg, a helicopter ride from Salt Lake City to Logan. The helicopter landed in the center of the Utah State University campus, a mile from the mouth of Logan Canyon. Hatch stepped out, opened the box with a penknife, and presented Old Ephraim's remains to the university.

Today, Old Ephraim's 15-inch skull—no longer so powerfully aromatic—lies in a glass-sided "Sleeping Beauty case" in the basement of the Merrill-Cazier Library. The left fang and eye socket are missing, scorch marks have blackened the bone above the molars, and metal staples hold the back of the skull in place. An identification number, 243406, is scratched into the snout. About once a day, a visitor asks to see Clark's trophy. For a while in 2006, curators removed the skull from prominent display while using its case for another, temporary exhibit. They said if they failed to return the skull to a place of honor, there'd be "riots."

They exaggerated, of course. But inflating legends has been the norm for the West, where adding one's own dramatic bits to a story enhances the telling. Frank Clark told of killing Old Ephraim when prompted, but historian Frank M. Young, who interviewed Clark many years later, said the big, sinewy shepherd "never boasted of his exploit." However, writers and campfire tale-spinners practically have turned Clark and the last grizzly into David and Goliath. Old Ephraim gets nastier, Clark more fortunate. Utah's last grizzly lives on in books, tourist pamphlets, paintings, and a huge stone marker atop his grave, not to mention the names of a mountain man club and a biking and hiking trail. It's no coincidence that Logan High School students adopted "The Grizzlies" as their nickname in 1925, two years after Old Ephraim's death.

MULE'S-EAR WYETHIA,
NAMED FOR THE SHAPE
OF ITS LEAVES AND
FOR EXPLORER N. J. WYETH,
WHO TRAVERSED THE
CONTINENT IN 1834,
CARPET THE GROUND
NEAR TEMPLE FORK.

Clark might not approve of the fuss. "If I had to do it over again, I wouldn't do it," Clark told his niece. He felt remorse over killing such a magnificent animal. For many years, he visited the grave each summer. On a nearby tree he nailed a board painted with the words, "Here lies Old Ephraim. He gave Frank Clark a good scare."

Logan Canyon, in northernmost Utah, has much in common with Old Ephraim. Similar to the giant grizzly, it is among the last of its kind. If not the West's last unspoiled place, Logan Canyon—with its alpine wildflowers, limestone cliffs, rushing trout streams, and myriad other signatures of nature upon unsullied canvas—remains something to be treasured and preserved.

And like the tale of Old Ephraim, Logan Canyon needs no embellishment to secure its place in Western lore. It is not so deep as the Grand Canyon. It lacks the moonscape starkness of Arches or Canyonlands National Parks. It can't match Yellowstone for geologic grandeur or range of big animals. Yet its quiet charm never fails to amaze. As the sagebrush oceans of the Great Basin give way to big-box stores, multilane highways, and housing developments that creep up the mountainsides, replacing deer and cougar with streetlights and multicar garages, the beauty of Logan Canyon gains importance.

Logan Canyon "is how we know where we are in the world," said Utah naturalist Tom Lyon.

Walking along a trail studded with Indian paintbrush and columbine. Sitting amid the juniper or fir, miles from another human. Listening to the sparkling Logan River crash over boulders on its way to Cache Valley to the west. Smelling the sweet, moist earth of spring and the tang of conifer in the winds that race down the slopes. These are simple—some would say spiritual—experiences beyond price. The crown of trees over the highway near Wood Camp, where Mormons cut timber for railroad ties more than a century ago, forms "a green tunnel, it's like going to heaven—just lush, just sylvan," said Nancy Williams, a Logan bird-watcher who decided to attend Utah State University after driving the verdant tunnel four decades ago. Forty-one miles of national scenic byway bifurcate the canyon and surrounding Wasatch-Cache National Forest. U.S. 89 allows access to the breathtaking beauty but remains almost entirely unscarred by commercial development.

Historian Frederick Jackson Turner, famous for espousing the importance of the frontier in American development, fell under

Logan Canyon's spell when he visited northern Utah to teach college and fish for trout in the mid-1920s. He wrote his wife about the quaking aspen, the splashing river, and the "bluest gem of a lake"—Bear Lake, sometimes called the Caribbean of the Rockies—that lies below the canyon's eastern edge. Watching from his room at Utah Agricultural College (now Utah State University), he proclaimed the country "quite a perfect Paradise."

"At night I sleep under one or two blankets," Turner wrote in late June 1924. "The wind blows in a cold stream from the canyon into my room all night. The moon is so radiant as it rises full over the mountains that you can hardly look long at it without being dazzled, and the sunsets over the mountain rim are gorgeous. The meadowlarks sing beautifully."

Visitors often seem surprised. But that has long been the norm for Utah. The *Deseret News,* a Salt Lake City newspaper older than the *New York Times,* noted in 1891 how artists and writers rushed to enshrine the beauty of Colorado, California, Oregon, Washington, and the Yellowstone country of Wyoming but ignored Utah.

The pattern of American settlement explains much. Lewis and Clark missed Utah to the north. Fur trappers stumbled into northern Utah 20 years later but didn't stay. Euro-Americans settled the Great Plains and then leaped the so-called Great American Desert beyond the 100th meridian to pan for gold and plow the earth of the Pacific coast. Not until two events—the Mormon settlement of the Valley of the Great Salt Lake beginning in 1847, and the completion of the transcontinental railroad at Promontory Point in 1869—did the world begin to take Utah seriously. Even afterward, southern Utah, eventual home of five national parks, grabbed most of the attention.

Logan Canyon's legend has remained small. Visitors don't expect such beauty as they drive toward Yellowstone and the Tetons from Salt Lake City. While they appreciate the landscape outside the windshield, few stop to explore far from the pavement or to soak up the contours of human and natural history that make the canyon unique.

The canyon has quietly been home to splendors kept pristine by isolation. Species of violet and primrose grow here but nowhere else on Earth. Limestone depressions high in the mountains form pockets of air that register more than 60 degrees below zero Fahrenheit in midwinter. Huge rock walls rate among the most difficult climbs on the planet, ensuring their veneration by extreme sports enthusiasts. Mountain lions and moose pop into the valley for a look around, only to disappear into the

canyon forests again. Here too are Utah's version of the Blair Witch and a recently discovered cave system that may include America's deepest limestone cavern.

To tour Logan Canyon is to step back into the spirit, if not the look and feel, of the Old West. And there is no better place to start than history's biggest river.

MILE MARKER 461

"C'mon, Taylor!" Dee Taylor called to an excitable black-and-white retriever.

It was the day after Thanksgiving, a postcard day for a hike. The sapphire sky stung the eyes. Early snow clung to the cliffs, and the air along the Bonneville Shoreline Trail had the clarity and metallic taste of approaching winter.

The trail, which slices across the mouth of Logan Canyon, had been marked by earth-moving equipment, which left a gray-red scar amid the juniper, sage, and maples. Rocks from marble- to Volkswagen-size lay scattered throughout the soil like fruit cocktail in gelatin. During the dry season from May to August, foot-

SHOSHONE WOMEN, ROBED AND BLANKETED, CROSS LOGAN'S TABERNACLE SQUARE IN 1909. MORMON COMMUNITIES SPROUTED IN THE 1860S ON LAND WHERE THE SHOSHONE HUNTED BIG GAME AND PICKED CHOKECHERRIES.

steps on the chalky conglomerate stir up clouds of dust, but autumn rains and an early snow transformed it on this day into half-congealed concrete. A misstep would mean catching a toe and sprawling headfirst.

On a level stretch Dee Taylor looked up.

Mendon Peak and the Wellsville Cone, in the Wellsville Mountains ten miles to the west, seemed close enough to touch. Scoured channels in the peaks, spoon furrows in vanilla ice cream, indicated ancient glaciers. The mountains' sharp sides,

A PATENT MEDICINE AD
FROM A CENTURY AGO,
REGULARLY REPAINTED,
ADORNS A LANDMARK
BARN SOUTH OF LOGAN.
EVEN WITHOUT DR. R. V.
PIERCE'S DEFUNCT PRE-
SCRIPTION, UTAH RANKS
THIRD AMONG STATES IN
LIFE EXPECTANCY,
ACCORDING TO THE
CENSUS BUREAU.

looking as if clawed by some gargantuan beast, alternated between snow on the northern slopes and sun-drenched bare rocks on the southern exposures. Stripes of light and dark marked the Wellsvilles, one of the steepest ranges on the planet, like the flanks of a zebra.

At the mountains' feet lay Cache Valley, a collection of farms and towns originally organized as settlements on the orders of Brigham Young, the Moses of the Church of Jesus Christ of Latter-day Saints (Mormons) who led his followers to Utah to escape religious persecution. The *Deseret News,* Young's church-owned paper, got it right when it described the valley in 1859, the year of the first permanent white outposts: A "beautiful and pleasant" land of abundant water, wood, and grass.

Closest to the Bonneville trail was Logan, the county seat. The double towers of the city's Mormon Temple rose above the homes and downtown buildings. Their bright white cupolas stood out amid the browns and grays of streets, roofs, and dormant trees.

Above the temple, closer to the mouth of Logan Canyon, perched the campus of Utah State University and the still verdant fairways and greens of Logan Golf and Country Club. The two-mile segment of Bonneville trail to the east of the university skirted the back nine and an irrigation canal as it wound from Green Canyon southward to a neatly manicured tee box above the entrance to Logan Canyon. Then the trail descended to the Logan River and the highway paralleling it. Across the pavement, above a duck pond and volleyball court, another section of trail followed a game fence south. Beyond Cache Valley's southern boundary, the Bonneville trail picked up again and extended dozens of miles on and off through Weber, Davis, Salt Lake, and Utah Counties.

Taylor wagged her tail, lifted her nose from a clump of sagebrush, and trotted back to the group.

Out for the exercise were Dee, an affable, dark-haired man in his 50s who favors Clark Kent eyeglasses and a good Cabernet; his daughter; her two children; and two friends along for their first trip on the trail. Dee acknowledged it's a bit odd to have a family dog that shares his last name, but Taylor came from a shelter with tags already filled out. The name was a serendipitous fit, a sign the mutt was right for the family. Dee hikes the trail often, and Taylor, as friendly with strangers as the rest of the family, keeps time on their outings with the four-beat slap of her paws.

Dee Taylor pointed a few hundred feet above the trail to a stone cathedral known as Castle Rock. He recalled the summer day a decade ago when he tried to climb to the top of the Bear River mountains to scatter his father's ashes. That was before he gave up cigarettes, he said, and he couldn't catch his breath.

"I got as far as Castle Rock," he recalled. "I said, 'Dad, this is as high as we're going to go.'" He released the gray grit into the wind.

"For the rest of that summer, Castle Rock was colored with ash."

The trail, the rocks, and the mountains are old friends to those, like Dee, who live beneath them. The sun hides the valley in shadow each morning before it pops above the Bear River Range,

and again at night as it lingers behind the Wellsvilles. On a clear day, hikers can see James Peak, home to the Powder Mountain ski resort, to the south and the Malad and Bannock ranges of southern Idaho to the north.

"We have excellent light," said Logan resident Colleen Howe, who grew up in Montana and now makes a living selling her pastel paintings of Cache Valley, Logan Canyon, and other landscapes. "Sometimes the light hits the tops of the mountains, and filters through, peeking through the bottoms of the clouds. The light is vibrant and varied … and the clarity! Sometimes I wake up and feel as if there is nothing between the sun and me."

The land bears the imprint of the geologically recent Lake Bonneville, more ancient oceans, and even older mountain ranges. Rocks lying exposed near the Idaho border contain fossils of the great Cambrian "explosion" of 500 million years ago that gave rise to a broad range of complex, multicellular animals in a small window of geologic time. About 350 million years ago, northern Utah lay under a warm, shallow sea near the Earth's Equator. Layers of sedimentary limestone and fossils of tulip-like crinoids, horn corals, and trilobites bear testimony from atop high peaks to the pressures that formed Utah's rugged mountains through uplifts, depressions, and faults acting on the seafloor.

LOGAN RESIDENT DEE TAYLOR AND HIS HIKING BUDDY, A DOG ALSO NAMED TAYLOR, REST AFTER CLIMBING TO CASTLE ROCK ABOVE THE BONNEVILLE SHORELINE TRAIL. THE TOWN OF LOGAN LIES BELOW.

PRECEDING PAGES:
AUTUMN TOUCHES
THE MAPLES OF
MAPLE BENCH IN THE
WELLSVILLE MOUNTAINS,
FOREGROUND. CACHE
VALLEY STRETCHES TO
THE BEAR RIVER RANGE
IN THE DISTANCE.

Western and northern Utah lie in the Great Basin, a huge, intermountain bowl. Mountain ranges in the basin sprang up as blocks of rock, tilted and aligned north-south along fault lines. Geologist Clarence E. Dutton examined the first accurate terrain maps of the basin more than a hundred years ago and said the scattered ranges looked like an "army of caterpillars" crawling either toward or away from Mexico. Two of the north-south woolly worms are the Wellsville Mountains and the Bear River Range, both extensions of the Wasatch Range that played host to the 2002 Winter Olympics.

In the 1870s, geologist Grove K. Gilbert observed evidence of an ancient, giant lakebed in the basin and named the lake for an earlier explorer, Capt. Benjamin Louis Eulalie de Bonneville.

The northern Great Basin's valley floors, including Cache Valley, caught the water that formed Lake Bonneville and at least two earlier lakes during the most recent ice ages. The ghosts of Bonneville's shorelines still encircle Utah like bathtub rings. Lower rings mark the times when the lake level stabilized for a while before dropping and leaving only the Great Salt Lake, invisible on the other side of the Wellsvilles, as a remnant. At its peak, Lake Bonneville covered about 19,690 square miles, the size of Lake Michigan. The water drowned central Utah to a depth of more than a thousand feet and submerged everything

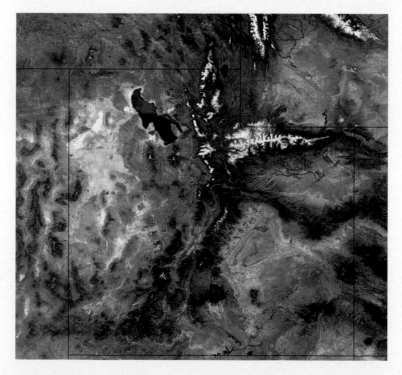

GREAT SALT LAKE, REM-
NANT OF THE ICE-AGE
LAKE BONNEVILLE,
APPEARS DARK BLUE
FROM SPACE. BONNEVILLE
COVERED THE LIGHT
TAN AREA OF WESTERN
UTAH; THE ARID WHITE
PATCH TO THE GREAT
SALT'S LEFT GETS ITS
COLOR FROM MINERALS
DEPOSITED WHEN
BONNEVILLE DRAINED
AND EVAPORATED THOU-
SANDS OF YEARS AGO.

in Cache Valley except the Bear River Range, Wellsville Mountains, the Malad and Bannock ranges, and the tops of Newton Hill and Cache Butte. The peaks stood dry like peninsulas and islands.

When Lake Bonneville formed in the ice ages, Logan Canyon looked much different than it does today. Fields of ice hid the mountaintops above 7,000 feet, and glaciers cut cirques and furrows that would become alpine meadows and U-shaped valleys in warmer times. Bristlecone pines, now gone, mixed with other conifers and spruce. Bears, woolly mammoths, and musk oxen populated the thick forests of the mountains and Willow Valley, the original name of Cache Valley.

A decline in evaporation rates and a slight increase in precipitation, coupled with the resulting increase in summer runoff, boosted Lake Bonneville's level during the last ice age. Also contributing to the lake's rise was the Bear River. Today it flows in a long, upside-down "U" around the mountain range that shares its name as the river makes its way to the Great Salt Lake. The modern Bear River's journey from source to mouth is about a 75-mile trip as the crow flies, but 500 miles by canoe. The Bear once flowed north into the Snake River, but volcanic activity, which created Idaho's Lava Hot Springs, dammed the river and sent its waters south. The redirected river cut a channel and entered Cache Valley about 27,000 years ago. As Great Basin lakes have no drainage—even today, water that flows into Great Salt Lake leaves only through evaporation—the addition of the Bear River's waters accelerated Lake Bonneville's growth.

Bonneville reached its highest level about 18,000 years ago. At that point, the shoreline lay about 5,100 feet above sea level. Logan would have been under hundreds of feet of water.

Then, about 14,500 years ago, Lake Bonneville's level dropped. Catastrophically.

Like the Great Basin's mountain ranges and valleys, the lake stretched mainly north-south. A keen observer, Gilbert noted how Bonneville's 2,000-mile shoreline rose higher near the longitudinal center, where the water had been deepest, than at the lake's shallower northern and southern fingers. Near today's Great Salt Lake, the Bonneville shoreline ranges from 5,160 feet to 5,230 feet above sea level. In southern Idaho, the bathtub ring rests at 5,100 feet. As water always seeks its own level, Gilbert surmised that the weight of the lake had depressed the Earth's crust, like a heavy body on a soft mattress. Sudden lifting of the load had caused the surface to snap upward. Such "crustal rebound" was more pronounced where the water's depth and weight were greatest.

PRECEDING PAGES:
THE LOGAN RIVER,
PARALLELING U.S. 89,
SPREADS OUT BEHIND
THIRD DAM TO FORM A
POPULAR FISHING HOLE.
THE LATE-AFTERNOON
VIEW FACES WEST FROM
THE CRIMSON TRAIL.

Gilbert wondered: What had caused the sudden emptying of Lake Bonneville? He sought clues in the rocks and published his findings in 1890. His description of the lake and its disappearance became "Monograph No. 1" of the U.S. Geological Survey.

His conclusion: Mother Nature pulled the bathtub plug.

At the northern end of the lake, a wall of sediment and stone precariously held Bonneville in check. Erosion from the headwaters of Idaho's Marsh Creek ate into the earth-and-gravel plug from the north, and water pressure from the lake pushed from the south. The wall exploded outward at what is now Red Rock Pass on U.S. 91 near Preston, Idaho, northwest of Logan Canyon. Bonneville's contents poured out at the rate of 15 million cubic feet per second, about four to five times the flow of the Amazon at its mouth, and spilled down the Snake River to the Columbia and the Pacific.

The maximum current lasted only a few days, but the flow remained for a year. The churning channel crested at 400 feet at Portneuf Narrows, 45 miles from Red Rock Pass. It picked up basalt boulders as easily as lima beans and rolled them into mile-long piles along the Snake River Basin. Idahoans call them "petrified watermelons."

Scientists haven't found evidence of Indians living along the shores of Lake Bonneville when the dam burst; the first arrivals to northern Utah may have come hundreds of years later. However, if the earliest travelers who crossed the land bridge from Asia about 15,000 years ago had settled the Pacific Northwest by that time, they would have heard the crashing waters many miles away.

Lake Bonneville stabilized in Cache Valley at about 335 feet below its maximum height. Gilbert dubbed this level, which also cut beaches into Utah's mountainsides, the Provo Shoreline. The University of Utah, Brigham Young University, and Utah State University rest on shoreline deposits at the Provo level.

Further lowerings of the lake left more rings. When Dee Taylor stopped at the southern end of the Bonneville Shoreline segment above Logan Canyon and looked to the south, he observed deltas stacked one on top of another like stones in an Aztec ziggurat. Looking up, he saw the shoreline looming above the pavement of U.S. 89.

Today, those who walk along the Logan River from the canyon mouth, following its meanderings toward its rendezvous with the Bear River, see the remnants of old deltas. Each is partially intersected by newer ones. The Mormon Temple sits on one of the most beautiful deltas, and downtown Logan on two more. Likewise, to the north and south, other streams flowing west out of the Bear River mountains formed their own deltas. Today, these "benches" ring the valley and provide hikers with panoramic views.

Dee stopped for a few minutes above the golf course and drank in the entire valley. A hawk circled overhead, and deer pellets lay scattered at his feet. Summer's old grass stood stiff, the color of straw. Winter would come soon, followed by green shoots and wildflowers in spring. Allowing for the occasional earth-shattering event, things change at nature's pace in the Bear River mountains.

Maybe Dee thought of that, as he turned for home and passed beneath Castle Rock and the ashes of his father.

MILE MARKER 463

Upon entering Logan Canyon, visitors encounter a series of small dams within the first five miles. Like the local governments' efforts to improve and extend the Bonneville trail, the dams reveal how human character can shape the landscape.

Utahns are by nature a conservative lot—consider, for example, that the town of Randolph, not far from Logan Canyon's eastern exit, gave George W. Bush 95.6 percent of its vote in the

THE BEAR RIVER, FLOW-ING NEAR THE BANNOCK RANGE, LED PATHFINDER JIM BRIDGER IN 1824 TO THE GREAT SALT LAKE, WHICH HE MISTOOK FOR THE PACIFIC OCEAN.

A MUNICIPAL POWER
PLANT, ITS TAILRACE
ABOVE, WAGED A PRICE
WAR WITH A PRIVATE
SUPPLIER OF ELECTRICITY
WHEN THEY BOTH
OPERATED ON THE
LOGAN RIVER EARLY IN
THE 20TH CENTURY.

2004 presidential election—and they shun ostentation in place-names. Streets in Utah towns are numbered in an X-Y grid. Dams in Logan Canyon are named First, Second, and Third, starting at the bottom and working up.

The turbine at Second Dam generates up to 15 percent of Logan's electrical power. A century ago, the city built a power plant there to compete with the privately run Hercules Power Co. at the canyon's mouth. The push for a publicly owned power system began in 1902, when Logan residents complained about Hercules' exorbitant rate of $1.25 per month for one lightbulb and 50 cents for each additional light. The private company had a monopoly and told the critics to shut up and pay up. Logan's mayor responded by calling a bond election. Citizens voted to spend $65,000 to erect a municipal dam and power plant to compete with Hercules. Construction was well under way in the summer of 1903, near the site of the Logan River's first sawmill, when Hercules suddenly decided to raise its dam five feet.

"The apparent purpose was to flood a much larger area, which would thus include the area where the new city power building was being constructed," historian Leon Fonnesbeck said. Water backed up onto the municipal power building's floor. When the town of Logan protested, Hercules smugly said it had planned to raise its dam for some time, and wasn't it a shame the city hadn't checked first.

Logan filed a federal application for rights to the site of its powerhouse, only to be told that Hercules had filed a claim ten days earlier. Both sides pointed fingers, and the Interior Department eventually compromised by authorizing two dams on the river that did not interfere with each other. The result: On May 4, 1904, Logan welcomed two competing electrical systems. The city's streets had two sets of electrical lines and poles, while surrounding towns and farms, independent of Logan's power grids, had one or none.

Although the cat's cradle of power lines marred the city's beauty, the sudden competition touched off a rate war. The City Light Plant charged 35 cents for a customer's first electric light, or three lights for a dollar. Logan's private competitor dropped its rate to 20 cents per light, and then 10 cents. City Light matched the price. Until metering began in 1927, Logan blazed like modern Las Vegas. Users paid by the lightbulb or appliance, not by how long they operated.

"Logan was a city which flowed freely with electricity," Fonnesbeck said. "The front porch light burned all night, as the price was the same."

Power company employees known as "checkers" determined bills by knocking on doors and counting lightbulbs, toasters, and other electrical devices. Many residents hid their appliances when they heard the knock. Students at the university, aware of the hide-and-seek game, commonly cheated the despised checkers and got a month's worth of electricity for as little as a dime.

MILE MARKER 464

Near Second Dam and east toward Third Dam, a series of limestone cliffs supports a population of rare flowering plants. Maguire's primrose, named for a longtime botanist at the New York Botanical Garden, grows only in Logan Canyon, and only in cracked limestone formations in the lower third. In late April and early May, the primrose flowers burst forth like the Hanging Gardens of Babylon in the moist, north-facing rock walls. Blossoms are delicate, beautiful, pink-to-purple, and fragrant if you get close enough to smell them.

"You've got to be a little nimble to be close," observed Mary Barkworth, director of the Intermountain Herbarium, a library of images and dried plants at Utah State University. "And they don't encourage it"—they being the U.S. Forest Service. Rock climbers had many of their favorite runs declared off-limits when the service discovered the routes ascended directly over primrose sites.

Frank "Buddy" Smith, a Cache Valley botanist, often hires out to government agencies and private companies to do baseline studies of plants and ecosystems at risk from encroaching human populations. For weeks at a time he hikes in the West, somewhere off the usual path, observing plants. When he's done, he's not keen on hiking the canyon for fun; he'd rather relax in New York, Chicago, or San Francisco and soak up the abstract art he loves.

"When you're a botanist," he said, "you might be an artist in a way because you're looking at colors and shapes."

Smith went looking in Logan Canyon in 1989 for two rare combinations of shapes and colors, the Cronquist daisy and Rydberg's musineon, when he found something completely new: a violet surprisingly growing at face level out of the limestone of Mill Hollow, between Second and Third Dams. When he looked up, he saw others in the sheer cliff face. "I collected it but I didn't think too much of it at first," Smith said. "Finally I tried to key it out at the herbarium. I looked through all the collections and thought, 'I must be missing something in the key.'" He kept coming back to the flower's short, lime green spur, which didn't match any description. Smith showed the flower to botanist Noel Holmgren of the New York Botanical Garden. Holmgren did his own examination and told him, "Buddy, this is a new species." Since then, as many as 10,000 *Viola frank smithii* plants, named for their discoverer, have been found—again, exclusively in Logan Canyon.

Each spring, Smith has no trouble talking himself into hiking to visit the rich clusters of blue-purple petals that bear his name.

MILE MARKER 465

Not far from where Frank Smith found his eponymous violet, Logan Canyon's walls widen and its floor spreads, if only for a bit. What was a grassy meadow for picnickers more than a century ago has become a lush pond and riparian area of willows and cattails through the construction of Third Dam at Spring Hollow. Mallard ducks, golden eagles, kingfishers, hummingbirds, herons, and the occasional bald eagle hunt for food in the hollow, as do porcupines, beavers, muskrat, and mule deer. A "living fossil" defies time in the clear water—the horsetail, or snake grass, a jointed plant with hollow stems that flourished 400 million years ago. Silica collects in the plant's cell walls; Mormon settlers rubbed the stems inside pots and pans to scour the cookware clean.

The thick band of limestone above Spring Hollow reminded early visitors of a wonder of construction half a world away, earning it the name "China Wall." Weathering from wind and water carved an airy chamber amid the stone north of the highway, giving rise to an enduring legend. While the trail maps refer to the eroded stone formation as Wind Cave, local folklore designated it "Witch's Castle." It even supplied the witch.

"Hecate," said Professor Jeannie B. Thomas, director of Utah State University's folklore program. The old woman of Greek legend somehow has transformed into a supernatural, modern-day crone to terrify teenagers who park and spark. "She's this witch, and sometimes she has her son accompanying her. The big ritual is to go into Spring Hollow and chant her name, of course, and she comes out with her son, or with her dogs." Enchanted powers reported by Thomas's students include Hecate's ability to kill car engines.

"Freudians would have a lot of fun with this," Thomas said. "An adolescent boy goes up there and is faced with a woman who makes his car inoperable."

Thomas finds a scholarly center to tales of the canyon's witch. Hecate is a metaphor for the dangers that lurk just beyond the teen years. Kids like legends, she said, and it's fun to think about things beyond the physical world. Hecate's place at Third Dam may date to the 1920s, when the Mormon Church built a girls' lodge, now long gone, or to imaginations run wild in a wild landscape.

Despite logical explanations, Hecate folklore has been passed on for generations. Sightings of an old woman with long white hair and a long pale dress have been cataloged and filed in the university's folklore collection, including one related by Rulon Jones, a

FLOATING A CANAL OFF THE LOGAN RIVER IN THE LOWER CANYON PROVIDES COOL RELIEF ON THE HOTTEST OF SUMMER DAYS.

WIND CAVE, HIGH ABOVE
THE FLOOR OF LOGAN
CANYON, MOANS WHEN
A BREEZE FLOWS OVER
ITS OPENINGS, GIVING
RISE TO THE LEGEND
OF A RESIDENT WITCH,
NAMED HECATE.

Utah State football player who enjoyed a career with the Denver Broncos. One particularly vivid version, from a driver identified only as "Clyde," told of a pickup truck that died in the middle of the highway just as it approached an old woman standing in the road near Third Dam. The woman, wearing a long, gray coat, peered in the cab window while Clyde frantically tried to restart the engine. Not until the woman walked behind the truck did the engine turn over. As Clyde left, he saw the woman in his rearview mirror, "not running, just right behind the truck following it." As soon as the truck left the canyon, the face disappeared.

Logan native Troy Oldham, a public relations instructor at the

university, heard Hecate's story while attending a Boy Scout camp in the 1970s. As the scouts set up camp, he went fishing at Third Dam and looked across the road to the China Wall. "You look up, and there's a place that looks like a cave with little crosses, almost a ladder," Oldham remembered. "And I said, 'It looks like a little cave up there,' and somebody said, 'Yeah, it's Hecate's cave.'" Oldham asked an older kid if he had heard of Hecate, and the boy told him of a recluse driven out of Logan in the 1920s.

"'And at night you can hear her dogs howling,'" Oldham recalled the boy saying. "The natural phenomenon behind it is, when the night canyon wind blows through the caves, it sounds

THE DELECTABLE CHOKECHERRY

Chokecherries constituted a staple of the Shoshone diet. They bloom riotously in the lower parts of Logan Canyon and in southern Cache Valley in spring, sending forth fragrant wands of tiny white flowers. By fall, the flowers morph into dark, red fruit, which the Indians harvested and dried for winter. Naturally tart, if picked too soon the chokecherry fruit practically withers the tongue. Patty Timbimboo Madsen recalled her grandmother making a chokecherry porridge. The key, Madsen said, was to pick the fruit just as it got ripe. That is, if you could beat the birds, bears, and rodents who were waiting for exactly the same moment. Humans shouldn't eat the raw leaves and seeds: They contain hydrocyanic acid. Drying or boiling the fruit will neutralize the acid and sweeten the flavor.

THE CHOKECHERRY'S WHITE WANDS OF FLOWERS TURN INTO DARK RED FRUIT.

A MODERN TWIST ON A SHOSHONE FAVORITE

CHOKECHERRY PEACH JAM

2 cups peaches, finely chopped or crushed
2 cups chokecherry juice
1/8 cup lemon juice
5 1/2 cups sugar
1 package pectin
1/2 teaspoon butter

Combine prepared fruit and lemon juice in a 6- to 8-quart saucepan. Measure sugar into a separate bowl. Stir pectin into fruit mixture. Add butter. Bring mixture to a full rolling boil, stirring constantly. Stir in sugar quickly. Return to full rolling boil and boil exactly one minute, stirring constantly. Remove from heat. Skim off any foam. Ladle into washed and sterilized jars, filling to within an eighth of an inch of the tops. Cover with two-piece lids. Process jars in a hot water bath for ten minutes (adjust time for your altitude). Let stand at room temperature for 24 hours. Store in a cool, dry, dark place. Makes 3 to 4 pints.
—*recipe by Utah native Christine Anderson*

like the howling of dogs.

"I couldn't sleep that night."

On Memorial Day 2003, photographers captured the image of two women all in white above Spring Hollow. While their appearance may have shocked much of the valley, there was indeed a logical explanation.

When people curiously inquire who wore the white dress at their commitment ceremony—Lauri Muller and Andrea Griffiths call it a marriage, although Utah most likely would be the last state to recognize the joining as such—they reply, "We both did."

"We wrote our own vows," Muller said from her living room in Logan, where her life partner had just served hazelnut coffee and carrot-cake cookies to a guest. "We had a unity candle, but it was hard getting it lit in the wind."

Muller grew up in Nebraska and got sidetracked at the start of a college soccer career. She worked at church camps and moved to Logan to start classes at Utah State. Griffiths grew up a Mormon in Cache Valley and tried some online business classes before switching to nursing studies. A few months after they met, they became a couple. Then came deep conversations about faith and their life together.

A Protestant minister agreed to perform the couple's Logan Canyon ceremony. It included a reading of Corinthians 1:13, the Bible chapter that speaks of love as long-suffering, kind, and rejoicing. Communion featured nonalcoholic wine, a gesture to teetotaling Mormon friends and family among the 50 or so guests. Colorful wildflowers from the canyon and valley decorated the picnic area where Muller and Griffiths exchanged vows and rings. The two women had to speak up above the roar of spring snowmelt that was crashing down a creek toward the Logan River.

Perhaps more surprising than the ceremony was the reaction among those who learned of it in Cache Valley. Muller called it the "coolest thing" that lesbians would find support in pockets of conservative Utah, where the Mormon Church condemns homosexual actions while urging compassion for the actors. More so than in a lot of places where they've lived, Muller said she and Griffiths "found acceptance and love," particularly in the Presbyterian and Lutheran churches, but also here and there in the Mormon community.

As Muller and Griffiths shared a scrapbook of photos of their big day, they showed one of China Wall bathed in warm light. Beside it were the words, "The most beautiful view is the one I share with you."

THE FIRST VISITORS

There are no migration stories among the Northwestern Band of Shoshone. Oral tradition says they have *always* lived in the northern Great Basin.

How far back do the stories go?

"I would hear some of the elders talk about 'large creatures,'" said Patty Timbimboo Madsen, cultural and resource manager for the Northwestern Band. Nobody is sure what they were.

Madsen's local roots go deep. Timbimboo means "rock writer," a likely reference to the region's petroglyphs. Madsen also is the great-great-granddaughter of Sagwitch, a chieftain who converted to the Mormon religion. He and other Shoshone helped build the Logan Temple on a sacred Shoshone site.

Utah State University anthropologists have evidence of paleo-Indians in northern Utah around 13,000 years ago. Hundreds of campsites, kill sites, butchering sites, and tool-stone quarries indicate a hunter-gatherer culture. Population booms occurred about 9,000 years ago with the storage of hard seeds and the twin technological hallmarks of grinding stones and coiled basketry, and again about 1,000 or so years ago with the Fremont, a culture borne of farmer immigrants from the Southwest.

Indians used Logan Canyon as a highway. Chips found in the area of Idaho obsidian and Wyoming quartzite indicate people passing through, carrying trade goods or following

CHIEF WASHAKIE OF THE EASTERN BAND OF SHOSHONE HOLDS A TOMAHAWK AND POINTS TO THE DISTANCE DURING A DANCE IN WESTERN WYOMING IN THE 1880S.

game. "Their economy ran on tool stones as ours runs on oil," said Utah State anthropology professor Steve Simms.

A distinctive Shoshone culture emerged sometime between 1300 and 1500, although the region experienced considerable mixing of peoples from migration and intermarriage. The Shoshone called themselves Newe, or "The People," and moved with the seasons. In spring, they gathered roots and berries in

Cache Valley. In summer they collected grass seeds to prepare for winter meals. And in fall, when the rabbitbrush changed from pale green to yellow, they traveled to collect chokecherries and pine nuts, and to catch salmon to the north. Winter was a time for sewing, mending, and hearing the elders pass along ancient tales, many of which featured animals with human attributes who imparted lessons about the world.

"In our stories, the animals talked and interacted, and were humanlike," Madsen said. "My mother always said we had cartoons before other people had cartoons, because our animals talked." Shoshone creatures still talk. In 2005, the Northwestern Band published *Coyote Steals Fire,* a children's book depicting a trickster and his helpers who bring fire out of the desert. The Northwestern Band decided to tell the story

INDIAN SQUAWS WEARING ELK TOOTH ROBES FT HALL RESERVATION IDAHO

HEEBE-TEE-TSE, LEFT, FIXES HIS PROUD, STEADY GAZE IN AN 1899 STUDIO PORTRAIT. BY 1900, THE SHOSHONE HAD BEEN DEVASTATED BY DISEASE, WARFARE, AND LOSS OF ANCESTRAL LANDS TO WHITE SETTLERS. ABOVE, SHOSHONE WOMEN LINE UP ON HORSEBACK; AT RIGHT, A SHOSHONE WOMAN WEARS TRADITIONAL DRESS.

in English and Shoshone in hopes of helping preserve the dying language. Shoshone children drew the illustrations.

For centuries, the Shoshone hunted big game. Buffalo virtually disappeared from Cache Valley early in the 19th century, about a century after the horse's arrival facilitated the hunt. The reduction of game, along with the advent of European diseases and settlers who removed precious land from the food circuit, spelled hardship for the Shoshone.

"The threat came when the fences went up," Madsen said.

LAST UNSPOILED PLACE

TEPEES AT CACHE VALLEY'S FESTIVAL OF THE AMERICAN WEST, LEFT, SUGGEST THE WANDERING OF THE SHOSHONE. AT RIGHT, THE BEAUTY OF A QUIET RIVER BEND BELIES ITS VIOLENT PAST—HUNDREDS DIED IN THE 1863 "BEAR RIVER MASSACRE."

Mormon-Shoshone relations experienced violent flare-ups but fared better than many encounters between Euro-Americans and natives, partly out of a mutual desire to get along and partly out of religious sympathies. Brigham Young said he preferred to feed Indians than fight them. Furthermore, Mormons believe that Indians are the descendants of travelers who came to the Americas from the Holy Land around 600 B.C. Brigham Young called Indians "the seed of Israel through the loins of Joseph." Mormon religious practices—including an openness to revelations as well as, for a half century in the 1800s, polygamy—had Shoshone counterparts.

Despite good intentions, food grew scarce in Cache Valley by 1862. Raids on settlers' livestock, emigration trails, and supply trains to mines in Montana raised tensions, and skirmishes broke out. California's governor sent Col. Patrick Edward Connor to Utah to enforce peace.

Connor led nearly 300 soldiers into Cache Valley in January 1863. He did not intend to take any prisoners, Connor told a marshal who accompanied him on the journey north. Early on the bitterly cold morning of January 29, Connor's troops arrived where the Northwestern Shoshone were in camp on the Bear River. Connor, who had satisfied himself that these Shoshone were the ones responsible for the emigrant raids, ordered an attack. His soldiers surrounded the camp and killed

perhaps 300 to 400. Scores of women, children, and elderly lay among the dead. Sagwitch, shot in one hand, fled when the battle became hopeless. Connor lost 17 men. If the colonel later realized his mistake—he had identified the wrong group of Shoshone for retaliation—it probably did not bother his conscience. Connor had a well-documented faith in widespread violence as the best means to pacify the West.

It was the largest slaughter of Indians in a single battle with Euro-Americans west of the Mississippi River. The "Bear River Massacre" reduced the Northwestern Shoshone so brutally that it took nearly 150 years to regenerate the band to 455 enrolled members. The Northwestern Band keeps the memory alive with the number "1863" on its logo, and with subdued observances.

Patty Madsen quietly visited the massacre site on the 2006 anniversary date. Friends brought a prayer blanket and offerings of corn and fish to the spirits of her ancestors. It was a beautiful day, she said. The sun came out that Sunday afternoon as tribal elder Leland Pubigee offered a prayer.

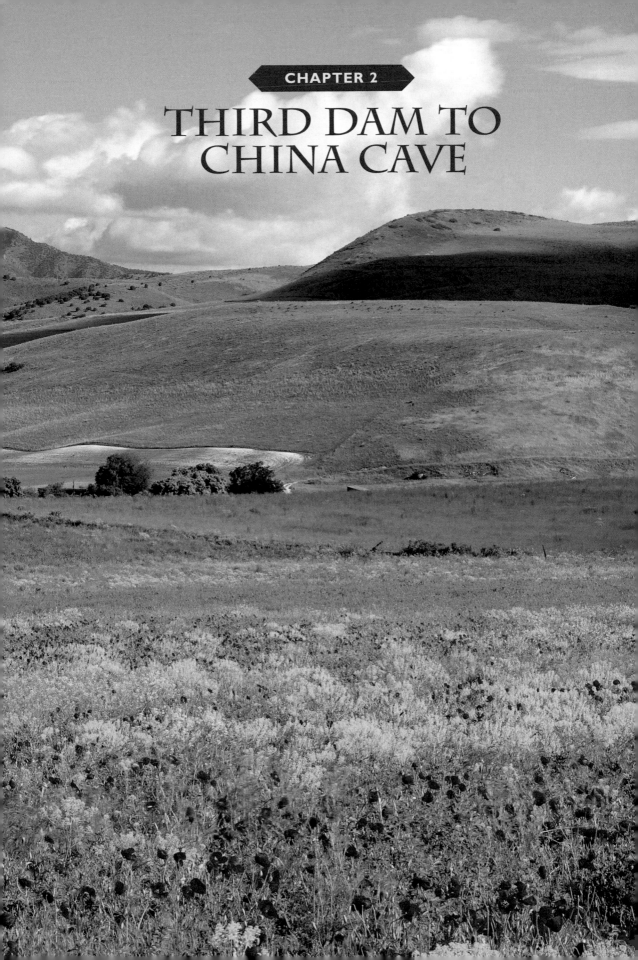

CHAPTER 2

THIRD DAM TO CHINA CAVE

LAST UNSPOILED PLACE

THIRD DAM TO CHINA CAVE

To a great extent, credit for preserving Logan Canyon's beauty belongs to two men named Roosevelt. The first one answered a petition from Cache Valley residents to protect their watershed, which had deteriorated so badly that one prominent, teetotaling Mormon publicly announced he might take up whiskey for his health. The second Roosevelt sent desperate young men, in a desperate time, into the canyon to carry out widespread, emergency conservation.

Warren Angus Ferris, the first Euro-American to enter Logan Canyon, described it as a place of "almost impenetrable thickets" in 1830. But within three-quarters of a century, the canyon had grown stunningly bare. A geology professor, William Peterson, had no idea how bad things had become when he set out on a 1903 survey of the Bear River mountains for the University of Chicago. "As I had known the area, the tops of canyons and the high cirques had never been grazed, so I started with a small amount of grain, feeling that I could graze my animals as the work proceeded," Peterson wrote. Instead, his packhorse and saddle horse found "absolutely no feed" on his first night out. He had to tie them up to keep them from wandering in search of food. "I purposely visited the very head of the canyons, those areas which were most generally inaccessible, but greatly to my surprise sheep had been there and had transformed what had previously been a luxuriant growth of grass and flowers into a dirty, uninviting barren spot." Other nights proved just as bad. Only once in his month and a half in the mountains could Peterson find enough grass for his horses to eat, and that required him to open a trail onto a ledge where sheep dared not go.

Surely, Peterson must have wondered, how could such devastation have happened?

It came slowly at first. The Shoshone and other Native Americans affected the ecology through hunting, gathering, and burning to encourage the growth of new grasses. Mother Nature also took a turn balancing the ledgers. Shoshone Chief Sagwitch recalled a terrible winter in the mid-1820s that killed all but

ICE AND FROST GLISTEN ON THE SURFACE OF THE LOGAN RIVER IMPOUNDMENT BEHIND THIRD DAM.

PRECEDING PAGES: RED POPPIES, A NATIVE OF ASIA, AND YELLOW DYER'S WOAD BLOOM ON THE WEST SIDE OF GUNSIGHT PEAK.

THE LOGAN, HYDE PARK,
AND SMITHFIELD CANAL
EMERGES FROM THE
MOUTH OF LOGAN
CANYON ABOVE AN EARLY
POWER PLANT. PIONEERS
CUT INTO SOLID ROCK
TO DIVERT WATER TO
THEIR FIELDS.

seven buffalo. The arrival of pioneers accelerated the alteration of Logan Canyon. After the establishment of the first permanent Mormon community in Cache Valley in 1859, settlers turned to the mountains for timber and water. Within a few years, sawmills buzzed to create hundreds of thousands of ties to connect local rail links to the transcontinental line, and canals diverted canyon water to farms and towns in the valley. Farmers moved their livestock into the mountains when their herds grew too large to manage on the valley floor.

The Logan River proved too wild for reliable transportation, and the rocky canyon floor delayed serious roadbuilding. Thus, rugged Logan Canyon was among the last bits of wilderness to be grazed. Seven brothers took the first herd of cattle into the canyon in 1873. Other Mormon settlers ran dairy operations in Logan Canyon, milking the cows, churning butter, and occasionally singling out livestock as currency to pay their church tithe.

Grazing and browsing seemed good uses for the unfenced land, which was too rocky and remote to support agriculture.

Livestock could be wintered in the valley and summered in the mountains. Cattle, which ate mostly grasses, reduced Logan Canyon's vegetation, but nothing like the sheep that became the valley's primary livestock in the last two decades of the 19th century, when the ovine population rose from 10,000 to 300,000. Sheep are primarily browsers, devouring broad-leafed plants along with the occasional bite of grass and sage. They stripped Logan Canyon like locusts in an Old Testament plague. Surviving photographs of the era depict sheep so thick on the mountainsides they hid the ground like snowdrifts. Their hooves packed the barren soil so nothing could grow. As they moved, they kicked up clouds of dust visible throughout the valley several miles to the west.

Without plant roots to hold back the snowmelt, spring runoff roared down the mountainsides instead of trickling all summer long. Muddy storm water, dead sheep, and animal waste polluted the Logan River, source of Logan's irrigation and drinking water. At a meeting of concerned Cache County residents in February 1902, Smithfield justice of the peace Moroni Price said the carcasses he observed in the mountain streams disgusted him so badly, "I have about reached a decision to drink whiskey from now on."

Residents of Cache Valley, realizing how much their canyon had deteriorated, debated whether to petition President Theodore Roosevelt to preserve the watershed by creating a "forest reserve" in the Bear River mountains. Not everyone favored the idea. According to a news account of the meeting at which Price made his pitch for whiskey over water, "Mr. Hobbs from Benson ... took the floor and indulged in a regular rip snorter of a talk. He thought the brush should be destroyed as it scratched his pants when he got out wood, and anyway, a timber reserve was a humbug. Prayer was the thing, just straight prayer and faith."

Despite Hobbs's plea, citizens voted overwhelmingly to ask the president to intervene. Roosevelt agreed to prevent the sale or settlement of land in the proposed reserve, and sent grazing inspector Albert F. Potter to Utah to perform a survey. Potter arrived in Logan on July 1, 1902, to analyze the grazing, timber resources, erosion, and watersheds of the Bear River mountains. With sheepherder Tom Smart, Potter rode into the high reaches of Logan Canyon on July 3, only to be turned back by a howling snowstorm. After the weather cleared, he saw much to convince him the locals were right: The canyon had been overgrazed and its timber overcut.

"Grazed almost to extinction," Potter wrote in his diary of the trip. "Barren of vegetation (especially around the river banks). It

A HIKER (INSET) SITS BESIDE A CANYON SPRING IN JUNE. LATER IN THE YEAR, THE SPRING SHOWS THE EFFECTS OF GRAZING AND LACK OF RAIN.

LAST UNSPOILED PLACE

would be hard to find a seedling big enough to make a club to kill a snake."

Potter took about 400 pictures during his survey, but only one remains in the possession of the U.S. Forest Service headquarters in Logan: "Lake Gog," as Potter called it, in midsummer. Comparison with modern photographs reveals the scene to be part of the alpine lake at Tony Grove, although today's visitors would be hard-pressed to believe it. The hillside in Potter's photograph appears nearly devoid of ground cover and supports only a handful of trees, unlike the explosion of fir, aspen, and wildflowers that now make Tony Grove one of the most popular camping and hiking spots in the canyon.

Acting on Potter's report, America's environmentalist president signed a proclamation creating the Logan Forest Reserve of more than 107,000 acres in May 1903. Fresh from a three-day wilderness trip through Yosemite National Park with renowned naturalist John Muir as his guide, Theodore Roosevelt underscored the need for preservation in a speech at the Salt Lake Tabernacle. America needed to protect its high timber country from being "devastated," he said to tumultuous applause.

"Our mountain forests must be preserved from the harm done by overgrazing," Roosevelt said. "Almost every industry depends in some more or less vital way, upon the preservation of the forests. And while citizens die, the government and the nation do not die, and we are bound to use such foresight in using our forests and ranges as will keep them for those who are to come after us."

The land set aside to preserve Cache Valley's watershed eventually shifted to the jurisdiction of the Forest Service and has become part of the nearly 1.3 million acres preserved as the Wasatch-Cache National Forest. The national forest, an archipelago of green oases stretching across northern Utah, covers more territory than Delaware.

I'm a firm believer that history teaches lessons," said Gary Anderson, chair of the steering committee of Cache Vision 2020+, a group of elected officials and interested citizens from throughout Cache Valley focused on long-term challenges such as population growth, water use, and pollution. "People who don't understand their history make the same mistakes over and over."

Anderson uses the example of the denuding of Logan Canyon a century ago, and President Roosevelt's subsequent creation of the forest reserve, to remind the valley's residents they're connected by ecology. He shows them news stories from 1902 while telling them, "It's déjà vu all over again."

ALBERT POTTER
CRADLES A WYOMING
ELK CALF IN 1918.
POTTER'S 1902 SURVEY
OF SHEEP-DEVASTATED
LOGAN CANYON PROMPT-
ED PRESIDENT THEODORE
ROOSEVELT TO CREATE
THE FORERUNNER OF
TODAY'S WASATCH-CACHE
NATIONAL FOREST.

Now air is as big a concern as water. Gases from motor vehi-
cles, wood fires, and dairy cattle flatulence occasionally get
trapped in Cache Valley by a midwinter inversion, an atmospheric phenomenon in which high, warm air traps a cooler air layer
below. The inversions are nothing new; the phenomenon led to
jokes a century ago. The *Millard County Progress* reported a fanciful
conversation in 1906 between two old-timers recalling a foggy
winter in Logan Canyon. "I seen it so all fired thick that we laid
abed for two whole days, supposing, of course, that it was night

LAST UNSPOILED PLACE

PRECEDING PAGES: SNOW
AND RIME ICE CLING TO A
DOUGLAS FIR AT THE
CANYON SUMMIT. FOG-
BLANKETED BEAR LAKE
LIES HIDDEN.

TONY GROVE LAKE,
LEFT, REFLECTS RUGGED
ROCK FACES IN EARLY
MORNING LIGHT. BELOW,
ALBERT POTTER'S "LAKE
GOG" PHOTOGRAPH
OF 1902, NAMED FOR NEAR-
BY MOUNT GOG, DEPICTS
THE SAME BODY OF WATER.

all the while," said one to the other, "on account of the fog bein'
so dense that daylight couldn't git thru it." The storyteller said he
cut some of the fog into blocks and buried it in sawdust "and
kept it until way in the summer."

In recent winters, Logan's winter inversions haven't been so
funny. They occasionally have made national news for contributing, for a few days at a time, to some of the worst air in America.
The roof of the valley's inversion-induced smog, when viewed
from above, corresponds roughly to the altitude of the
Bonneville Shoreline. A hiker in the high country on a February
day has little trouble imagining what Lake Bonneville would
have looked like.

BIGTOOTH MAPLES BLAZE
RED-ORANGE BENEATH A
CATHEDRAL OF LIMESTONE.
AUTUMN COLOR LURES
CROWDS TO THE LOGAN
RIVER IN LATE SEPTEMBER
AND EARLY OCTOBER.

"One hundred years later, we're trying to deal with gunk, we're trying to deal with the same problems," Anderson said. "The idea here is, our valley, our solutions. Let's deal with it before it gets so bad that somebody else has to come in and take over."

The Forest Service and ranchers of northern Utah have worked out their own compromises. By limiting the number of sheep and cattle allowed to graze in the Bear River mountains, the Forest Service has granted access without chaos. Summer cattle allotments permit 5,462 cow-and-calf pairs. Sheepherders have been granted 15 allotments to fatten 13,244 sheep over the summer.

Bret Selman, a sun-browned sheepherder with a black goatee and a blue gimme cap, runs his flocks on two 80-day allotments in Logan Canyon. His family has been in the sheep business for a century and received a canyon sheep permit in 1942. He is proud that his family's management of sheep allotments has helped bring the canyon back from the edge of ruin.

On a chilly morning in late June, Selman set out to move more than a thousand ewes and newborn lambs from a corral in Box Elder County to a shallow depression above Rick's Spring. His truck pulled up to the sheep pen just before 6 a.m. Dawn was merely a suggestion in the east, its first glow too weak to blot out the eggshell-sliver of a waning crescent moon and the white diamond of the morning star.

"Why, this is so early the coyotes ain't even up yet!" Jack Brown, Selman's main driver, yelled as he pulled up in the first of two livestock trucks.

"This is early?" deadpanned Selman, who had begun wetting the ground from a water truck. Sheep don't like to pass through clouds of dust, he explained, and might balk at being routed toward the transports if not for the buckets he emptied onto the dirt.

While Brown, Selman, and their helpers connected the chute with a ramp into the first truck, Selman's three children and uncle Dean began waving their arms and hollering to move the sheep. The family's border collies twitched and rocketed left and right. Jittery sheep crowded into the indicated corner of the lot and jostled each other. Meanwhile, Elké Selman, 12, and Peruvian shepherd Edwin Dionisio Flores, a compact man built like a wrestler, traded words in the kind of vocabulary lesson increasingly important to an industry that crosses cultural lines.

"Blue," said the girl, plucking the fabric of her sweatshirt.

"*Azul*," replied Dionisio Flores.

"Red." Elké pointed to the chute.

"*Rojo*."

Brown finished affixing a silvery metal ramp to the transport.

THIRD DAM TO CHINA CAVE

"Okey-dokey, Bret, let my little babies roll," he cried.

Ewes and lambs began filing into the wood-slatted chute leading to the ramp. As they passed, Selman examined each fuzzy backside for his family's registered zigzag identification mark. He said the red mark was a "Z" instead of an "N," explaining, "You read a sheep from the back." Sheep lacking the mark of Zorro had strayed from neighboring flocks; Selman segregated them into a pen to return them home.

"We've got a good set of lambs," Brown observed. "Broad and square like little pigs."

All of Selman's sheep would be sheared for a wool crop; many also would become someone's dinner. Shearing takes place around April 1 and slaughtering in the fall. Selman moves his sheep from winter range on a Bureau of Land Management site in the Hogup Mountains, near the Nevada line, to private land for lambing in the spring. Summer requires another move, to allotments in Logan Canyon and Wyoming. In fall, the sheep return to private land. The process makes a shepherd's life one of constant motion, not only to keep up with the change of seasons but also

SPRING SNOW DUSTS PASTURES IN CACHE VALLEY. DESPITE POPULATION GROWTH, THE VALLEY HAS REMAINED BUCOLIC.

LAST UNSPOILED PLACE

to round up strays. Selman uses a nifty trick to count his flocks. He keeps the ratio of white to black sheep at 50 to 1. That way, when the Peruvians who live with the sheep want to number them, they only need count the black ones and multiply by 50 to get an approximation.

With the trucks finally packed with sheep, the caravan to the unloading site got under way. The journey took just under an hour, during which the sun rose high and warmed the air. Half a century ago, shepherds on horseback needed seven days for such a trip.

It took another hour for men on horseback to get the sheep to climb a mile-long, aspen-filled gully to the allotment site. From there, still snowy peaks could be seen to the west through a frame of aspen branches and the petals of pink sticky geranium and yellow cutleaf balsamroot. Like all good shepherds, the men kept track of every sheep along the way. Bret discovered a neighbor's lamb and tied it to his saddle. It somehow had escaped the screening at the corral. Selman said he would return the newborn to its owner as soon as he could.

"If he had his mom, we'd just give him back in the fall," Selman said. "But he needs his mom."

The rest of the sheep, Z-backed, fanned out and settled in for the summer.

MILE MARKER 466

Cache County's youth answered the call of the second Roosevelt in the White House when America's economy lay in shambles and its wilderness faced new threats during the Great Depression. A federal agency created in 1933 by President Franklin D. Roosevelt had two main goals: To provide relief from record unemployment and to protect the nation's natural resources. The Civilian Conservation Corps employed a quarter-million down-on-their-luck Americans, especially young men with dependents. The work transplanted men from cities and towns to the countryside. Each man earned $30 a month, of which $25 went to his dependents at home. The CCC asked Utah for 2,300 enrollees; 400 people applied for positions on the first day. In Cache County, 275 young men applied for 113 slots.

Enrollees from all over the country planted trees, stocked fish, built dams and bridges, and fought fires in Utah. Two CCC camps opened in the Bear River mountains during the program's first year: Camp F-1, at Tony Grove in Logan Canyon, and F-2, in Blacksmith Fork Canyon to the south. The two camps combined after a year and operated until 1941.

The enrollees at Tony Grove wasted no time. Erected in the summer of 1933 on the site of a Utah State Agricultural College summer camp, F-1 boasted a mess hall, a recreation hall, four barracks, a blacksmith shop, a hospital, a shower building, and an administration building. Workers cleared roadsides, built rock dens to make fish ponds, and put up snowdrift fences.

Max J. Schlegel, a CCC worker who wrote a column for the Logan newspaper, said his work restored more than forests and fields. "Emergency conservation work is … a project essentially for restoring confidence, of building men through worthwhile work. … I have been given a chance to re-establish normal relations with life, to re-create faith in the future as well as the faith of relatives and friends, and an opportunity to send money home to help those who helped me and shared what little they had."

In their spare time, the youths at F-1 made belts out of snakeskins, posted an 11-1 record against local talent on the baseball diamond, and tricked newcomers into going on nighttime hunts to capture the mythical "snipe."

Logan Canyon enrollees included a contingent from distant states. For many, a summer in the western mountains had no equal in their experience. A New Jersey volunteer wrote with some exaggeration in an open letter published in the local paper, "They've got the workingest sun in this country you ever saw. Sunset don't come till almost midnight and then the sun gets up again about one o'clock in the morning and it makes it hard for me to get enough sleep." The letter writer, identified as "a C.C.C. boy," told his friend Bud, "I'm about seven shades browner than you saw me last."

CCC volunteers from the Deep South adjusted slowly to the steep mountain slopes, so unlike the humid lowlands of home. They made their feelings known when a Cache Valley church group traveled to the Tony Grove camp one night to direct a "community sing." The church singers began the program with "America." When they reached the line, "I love thy rocks and rills, thy woods and templed hills," comic groans arose from the flatlanders.

The CCC's legacy includes Guinavah-Malibu campground, a mile east of Spring Hollow. Jewel of the campground and picnic area is the thousand-seat Guinavah amphitheater, completed in 1936. The amphitheater, set half a mile from the highway, features a stage constructed of locally quarried limestone opposite rows of benches set into the mountain slope. Since it opened, the amphitheater has been in demand during summer for reunions, lectures, concerts, and religious services. Sitting in a grove of bigtooth maples visited by songbirds and mule deer, the amphitheater is a good place for groups to appreciate the canyon's scenery. Guinavah means "fish water" in the Shoshone language. That also is the Shoshone name for the Logan River.

"We are here to worship in God's creation, a simple beautiful place," Pastor Dave Hedgepeth told his flock in July 2004 during Logan First Presbyterian Church's annual summer service at Guinavah. The congregation had opened worship under a clear blue sky and a hint of a breeze by singing "Morning Has Broken" and "This Is My Father's World." "Here we are reminded that God's creation is good, and that we are part of something good," Hedgepeth added. His sermon, titled "Big Rocks," compared the limestone cathedrals that surround Guinavah to the most important priorities of a well-ordered life. Everything else is sand and gravel, he said.

In a heavily Mormon valley that is home to relatively few Protestants, sectarian lines get blurred out of necessity. The valley's Presbyterians drafted Hedgepeth—a Christian Church (Disciples of Christ) minister who married a woman raised in the Mormon faith—to spend two years in their pulpit while they sought a full-time Presbyterian pastor. As the congregation includes a plurality of people raised as Methodists, not to mention former Baptists,

PRESIDENT FRANKLIN D. ROOSEVELT, VISITING YELLOWSTONE NATIONAL PARK IN THE LATE 1930S, HELPED PRESERVE LOGAN CANYON THROUGH PROJECTS OF THE CIVILIAN CONSERVATION CORPS.

CCC OUTPOSTS, SUCH AS THE F-2 CAMP IN SOUTHERN CACHE VALLEY, DID VITAL WORK IN IMPROVING THE NATIONAL FOREST AND IN REBUILDING SPIRITS CRUSHED BY THE GREAT DEPRESSION.

Catholics, Lutherans, Mormons, and a smattering of other faiths, the job requires an open mind.

The valley's various congregations enjoy good relations. The Logan LDS Tabernacle regularly plays host to interfaith events, such as Christmas concerts and Thanksgiving services, and the Mormons pledged a sizeable donation to help pay for the Presbyterian church's renovation and expansion. That's a far cry from the late 1870s, when the fledgling Presbyterian congregation, the valley's second Protestant group, opened a day school that met with a measure of religious resistance. A Mormon furniture storeowner who rented space to the Presbyterians suddenly dissolved the lease and withdrew his children from their school after facing sectarian pressure. "People are mostly in sympathy with us," wrote Calvin Parks, the valley's first Presbyterian preacher, "except some spies, Episcopalians, and Mormons."

Despite initial reservations in the community, the church expanded its day school and added 64 members in Parks's eight years as pastor. Reconciliation followed. Charles O. Card, construction superintendent for Logan's Mormon temple, laid the foundation of the Presbyterians' first frame building. Other

denominations arrived and flourished, notably a Catholic church that has swelled in the last few decades through an influx of Hispanics, Utah's largest minority group.

MILE MARKER 467

Along the highway near Guinavah blooms the scourge of late spring. Dyer's woad, which produces an indigo dye, has an ancient history. Julius Caesar observed in his history of the Gallic Wars, "All the Britanni paint themselves with woad, which produces a bluish coloring, and makes their appearance in battle more terrible." Woad also may have been the source of the word "Pict," Latin for the Scottish people and derived from *picti*, meaning "painted."

In addition to inspiring fear in the enemies of Scotland, dyer's woad had medical and commercial applications. The Chinese mixed it into an herbal treatment for infections, and Albigensian merchants of the Middle Ages grew rich by coloring cloth with blue and blue-black dyes they drew from its leaves.

When European colonists introduced dyer's woad to the New World, it spread like a virus, particularly in the broken, dry landscape of the West. Left alone, one plant can shoot a taproot seven feet into the earth and produce thousands of purple-black seeds to be scattered by wind, water, and automobile tires. Seeds can survive for 15 years.

In May and June the herb, a member of the mustard family, grows three to four feet tall and produces canopies of tiny canary yellow blossoms. While beautiful, dyer's woad is an expensive invader, costing Utah millions of dollars in damage each year. Most animals, whether wild or domestic, won't graze it. Killing it can be a neat trick because if the top of the plant is plucked, the stem regenerates. Controlled burns can reduce populations, but fires also disturb the soil, creating ideal conditions for regeneration.

When dyer's woad replaces native ground cover such as sagebrush, the circle of life undergoes profound change. Rodents, grouse, and deer lose a portion of their habitat and seek food elsewhere. That affects coyotes, raptors, and other predators.

"People see that nice yellow plant in the springtime and they think, 'Oh, how beautiful,'" said Rob Cruz, district manager for the Logan Ranger District of the Wasatch-Cache National Forest. "But really, it's a noxious weed. It outcompetes the native vegetation the cattle prefer."

The Cache Valley Weed Department began paying youngsters to pluck and dig up the weed in a program whimsically named "Bag O' Woad." Kids got $10 per 40-pound sack. Demand was so high in 2002 that participants were limited to two bags each; still, the county had to seek additional funding to pay for the many tons collected.

If not for volunteers pulling and spraying the woad, "the whole canyon would be taken over," said Lisa Perez, the ranger district's conservation education coordinator. Rumor has it, she said, that all of the woad in northern Utah sprang from a plant that escaped from a woolen mill in Brigham City, just over the Wellsville Mountains from Logan. If the rumors are true, the Forest Service staff wonders, what might have happened if someone had uprooted that first fugitive before it could scatter its seeds?

In her home above Second Dam, Corinne Thul does her small part to keep woad from spreading. She picks the young plants in Logan Canyon as well as southern Cache County and turns them into indigo dye. The process takes about three hours, including chopping, seeping, and applications of ammonia to create an alkaline solution. Thul held up a glass jar containing the final result, a black dust resembling gunpowder.

"It makes me happy because even if I don't get my indigo out of it, it's a—well, I call it an 'ob'-noxious weed," Thul said. She planned to use the dye in a children's project at her church.

Cache Valley resident Tina Howard regularly makes indigo dye from the woad she collects along neighbors' fence lines. Applied to sheep's wool in varying amounts, it creates a permanent hue ranging from morning sky to navy blue. She knits mittens, hats, and sweaters from the colored yarn.

She probably will never have to worry about losing her supply.

"It reseeds itself so nicely," Howard said, summing up the Forest Service's lament about the invasive, hardy weed. "Generally if you have a spot with a little bit of woad, you'll have a lot next year."

MILE MARKER 468

Two miles east of Guinavah lies Card Canyon, named for the superintendent of Logan's temple construction. Hidden behind a limestone palisade and accessed by a bumpy dirt road that skirts overhanging walls of stone, the silent Card Canyon attracts big game. Hikers on a late-spring day encounter a checkerboard of deer and elk droppings, as well as cloven footprints in the mud near a churning rivulet.

CORINNE THUL, A LUTHERAN PASTOR WHO LIVES IN LOGAN CANYON, GATHERS AN ARMLOAD OF DYER'S WOAD AS THE FIRST STEP TOWARD PRODUCTION OF HOMEMADE INDIGO.

MOUNTAIN LIONS,
COUSINS TO THIS ONE
LIVING SOUTH OF UTAH,
ROAM THE BEAR RIVER
RANGE IN SUBSTANTIAL
NUMBERS, REMAINING
OUT OF SIGHT UNLESS
THEY CHOOSE TO
SHOW THEMSELVES.

The evidence offers mute testimony to the resurgence of elk. Hunters killed the region's last known native elk in 1898, when five were shot in Card Canyon. A boosters club paid $300 to have a train car of 25 replacements shipped to Logan from Wyoming's Grand Teton Mountains in January 1916. Logan residents gawked as the elk were driven, a few at a time, into a crate atop a sled and pulled six blocks from the depot to Tabernacle Square. For the rest of winter, the elk lived inside the tabernacle's fence at the intersection of Main and Center Streets in downtown Logan. Two of the beasts died in captivity, but the surviving 23 were set free in April and driven by a mounted posse into the mouth of Logan Canyon.

"No apparent problem was encountered on the drive since the elk seemed to naturally wish to move in the direction of the inviting hills," the Logan newspaper reported. "They traveled much as a herd of cattle do until they reached the old woolen mill on the canyon road, when something alarmed them and over the fences they went. It took a good while to get them back into the road again. ... The elk went up the canyon road as far as what is known as 'Jacky Hollow,' just this side of the second bridge, and then took up the mountain side."

Elk hunting resumed in 1925. A decade later the canyon held an estimated elk head count of 1,060. By the mid-1940s, the elk population had rebounded so strongly that the state established a ranch in Blacksmith Fork Canyon, to the south, to feed elk in the winter and keep them off cultivated land. Today, Hardware Ranch grows its own hay to sustain 500 to 600 elk during the snowy months.

Statewide, the elk population has increased tenfold since 1960, said Michael L. Wolfe, a Utah State University professor of wildlife ecology and management. Not so with deer, whose numbers have declined precipitously. There's no hard count—deer don't move in easily numbered herds, like elk—but anecdotal evidence, hunters' harvests, and low fawn-doe ratios all point to a decrease. Wolfe attributed the drop mainly to competition for forage with elk and moose, which are better able to find food in deep snow; an increase in predators such as mountain lions; and the loss of winter range to growing communities in Cache Valley.

Sitting in mid-February in his university office, Wolfe gestured out the window at an overcast, snowy afternoon that obliterated the Bear River mountains. "We've usurped the deer habitat," Wolfe said. When snow swallows the canyons, deer move into the valleys to seek food. They often find themselves channeled through new neighborhoods that push against the very edges of the steep mountain slopes.

"There's no place for the deer to hang out," Wolfe said.

As deer wander out of the mountains, they risk a close encounter of the vehicular kind. Mormon pioneers established towns throughout Cache Valley along deer migration routes. The valley's three main highways cut through those routes. Not surprisingly, automobile collisions ruin many a car while causing one in three deer fatalities in Utah.

But the danger is not just from cars.

Mountain lions, also known as cougars or pumas, carry out the natural world's version of Willie Sutton's law. An enterprising reporter quoted Sutton, a dapper 1930s hood, as saying he robbed banks "because that's where the money is." Mountain lions venture out of Logan Canyon into the farms and towns of Cache Valley because, when food becomes scarce in the high country, that's where the deer are.

"We've condensed the deer herd right in people's back yards, so why shouldn't lions hunt there?" Wolfe asked.

Wolfe is fascinated by the relationships among wolves, deer, elk, moose, bighorn sheep, and America's largest cats. Mountain

HOME SWEET HOME

Lutheran pastor Corinne Thul wakes up happy, feeling "closer to God" when she looks at the mountains from her rental home above Second Dam. But she's a malcontent compared with her 12-year-old Norwegian elkhound, Tor.

"His body quakes, as if he's saying, 'Are we going, are we going?'" Thul said of her dog's "addiction" to hiking in the canyon. "I go into the front room to turn on the radio, and he's so disappointed when I don't get the leash."

They regularly jog 1.5 miles along a trail about 50 yards from her door, then turn for the gentle climb back. It's one of the perks of living in Logan Canyon, along with the silence, the scenery, the wildlife right outside the window, and the nearly guilt-free eavesdropping that occurs when the mountainsides bounce hikers' voices over great distances.

Thul pointed out the hummingbirds and swallows that flitted near her lilac bushes, as well as her mustang grapes, cherry and apple trees, and an enormous freestanding fireplace she calls her "altar."

"I had wild turkeys," she said. "I called them my Gang of Five. They would charge me, and jump on my car, onto the bumper, and peck at my hood."

It was intimidating.

Thul found an advertisement for the home in the newspaper and snapped up the lease. The home was built to house the workers who maintained the power-generating equipment at the dam; after the house became empty, the Logan Light & Power Department went looking for a new tenant. The arrangement allowed Thul, a native of Minnesota, to fulfill a lifelong dream of living in a canyon.

MOUNTAINS MAKE A BEAUTIFUL BACKDROP FOR CANYON OR VALLEY LIVING.

When Thul moved into the home in late winter, the snow rested two feet deep. The sun became visible by late morning, she said, but elsewhere the narrow canyon hides winter sunshine for weeks at a time.

The canyon walls also block cell phone connections and broadcast television signals. Residents and visitors don't seem to mind. Some companies deliberately rent rooms in a high-canyon lodge for team-building exercises because they know participants won't be able to talk to anyone on the outside. Instead, they must focus their attention on whatever's at hand. Canyon life is slower, quieter, more introspective. By contrast, even sleepy Logan seems bustling.

In addition to a handful of ranger cabins and year-round residences, Logan Canyon is home to 84 summer lodgings on federally owned land. The U.S. Forest Service oversees the occupants' permits. Needless to say, there's not much turnover among permit holders.

lions can weigh as much as 200 pounds and grow as long as eight feet. They enjoy the greatest north-south range of any predator in the world, stretching from Argentina to Alaska.

From the time of the earliest pioneer settlements to the mid-20th century, Utah treated cougars as vermin and paid a bounty for each one taken. The animals finally received big-game protection in 1969, requiring hunters to obtain permits. Hunters now take 35 cougar each winter out of Logan Canyon, typically tracking them in snow and treeing or cornering them with dogs. Tracks often appear near an archery range in Card Canyon.

Mountain lions are heard more than seen in Logan Canyon, screaming in the distance. Longtime hikers tell novices that while they'll not likely see a cougar, the opposite is probably not true—the beasts silently watch human interlopers and show themselves only when comfortable doing so. Sheep may bring cougars out of hiding, and a few years ago Bret Selman had to kill one that visited his flocks.

Wolfe, who has taught in Utah for nearly four decades, said he has seen two cougars in the wild without the aid of dogs. One was a mother with a kitten south of Hardware Ranch; the other was chasing a deer in Box Elder County. He's also worked on a project to collar and track mountain lions in the Stansbury and Oquirrh Mountains west of Salt Lake City, to investigate their movements and project their impact on transplanted herds of bighorn sheep. Lines on a map on his office computer trace the cougars' wanderings. Surprisingly, one collared in the Oquirrh Mountains was killed more than 400 miles away in Colorado. Another traveled only about 80 miles, but the trip was notable for its destination. The cougar crossed I-15 and ended up in ritzy Park City, Utah, home of the Sundance Film Festival.

"We called him the Sundance Kid," Wolfe said.

A young male cougar caused a stir in summer 2003 when it calmly perched in a tree in a yard in Petersboro, on the west side of Cache Valley. Delores Yonk found the big cat 20 feet above the ground when her black Labrador, Molly, barked and woke her. The 80-pound lion lolled in the branches until wildlife officers shot him with tranquilizers and trucked him away.

"When people see a lion, they think there should be someone there to kill it," Wolfe said. While that may be true if the beast displays bold, dangerous behavior, most cougars that wander into human environments are merely confused. The vast majority of human encounters are nonfatal, Wolfe said, although the occasional death, such as a 1997 fatality in Rocky Mountain National Park, makes headline news.

THE LURE OF FUR

A fortune in furs and hides lured the first Euro-Americans into Cache Valley and Logan Canyon. They arrived a decade and half after Meriwether Lewis and William Clark, led by Shoshone guide Sacagawea, traversed the upper Rockies in search of a water route to the Pacific Ocean and information about the potential fur trade. Trappers working for the North West Fur Company entered Cache Valley in 1818, when a party of Canadians led by Michel Bourdon gave the Bear River its name. After Blackfoot Indians killed Bourdon west of Yellowstone, his companions honored him by affixing his name to another Cache Valley river. It didn't stick; later arrivals renamed the "Bourdon River" in tribute to another dead trapper, Ephraim Logan.

Beaver pelts, in demand for high-fashion hats, fetched high prices. Properly pressed and aired, pelts collected in the West were sold in St. Louis and shipped to New York for resale at a 1,000 percent markup. Explorers working for the Rocky Mountain Fur Company sought animal furs in northern Utah but found few beaver in the Bear River mountains. The rocky rivers moved

A TRAPPER DRAGS A DROWNED BEAVER FROM A UTAH POND. THE HUNT FOR LUCRATIVE BEAVER PELTS FUELED THE EARLY 19TH-CENTURY EXPLORATION OF THE WEST.

too swiftly to be corralled by beaver dams. Richer streams lay below, along the headwaters of the Bear River, where a party including Jim Bridger ran beaver traps in 1823. Bridger took a rawhide boat down the Bear River to where the stream emptied into a salty bay. Tasting the brackish water, he declared he had reached the Pacific Ocean. His error later became clear; Bridger's grave in Kansas City identifies him as "Discoverer of the Great Salt Lake."

Euro-American and Indian trappers came together throughout the upper Rockies beginning in 1825 in ever shifting gatherings known as rendezvous. Trappers wore clothing of animal skins, lived in tepees, cooked over campfires, and partied, frontier style. That typically meant horse races, wrestling matches, gambling, and shooting contests. Traders with connections to St. Louis paid the trappers cash for furs, allowing them to buy alcohol, coffee, sugar, and woolen cloth-

HUNTER, TRAPPER, AND TRADER JIM BRIDGER,
LEFT, EXPLORED NORTHERN UTAH AND
FAMOUSLY FEUDED WITH MORMON
PRESIDENT BRIGHAM YOUNG. HIS NAME
REMAINS PROMINENT IN CACHE VALLEY,
WHICH PROMOTES ITSELF AS "BRIDGERLAND."
THE CITY OF OGDEN, TO THE SOUTH, TAKES
ITS NAME FROM HUDSON'S BAY COMPANY
TRAPPER PETER SKENE OGDEN, RIGHT.

ing. The Cache Valley rendezvous in summer 1826 probably led to the construction of the valley's first wooden buildings, known as Camp Defiance, where a handful of hardy trappers spent the following winter. The site of the first Cache rendezvous remains the object of historians' debate, but the Old Ephraim Mountain Man Club places it at the mouth of Blacksmith Fork Canyon, near the modern town of Hyrum, south of Logan. During the rendezvous, mountain man Jedediah Smith and two partners, David E. Jackson and William H. Sublette, bought the Rocky Mountain Fur Company from William H. Ashley, a pioneering trapper who had organized the first rendezvous, at Henry's Fork in southwestern Wyoming, the previous year. The mountain men split up to hunt and trap in California and the Yellowstone country after the Cache rendezvous, but many returned to the valley for the winter.

The global market for beaver pelts declined around 1840, the last year of the Rocky Mountain rendezvous, as the fickle dictates of fashion swung in favor of silk hats. Independent-minded mountain men struggled to eke out a continued existence on the frontier. Some sold supplies and ferry rides to westbound migrants. Bridger, the most famous mountain man, turned mer-

chant and settled into his privately run trading post of crude log buildings on Black's Fork of the Green River. So-called Fort Bridger lay in Green River County, Utah Territory, but Wyoming gradually took control of the region and annexed it officially in 1868, drawing the boundary that forms the northeastern notch of modern Utah.

Bridger's trading post, situated where the Oregon and Mormon Trails split, served as a crucial place for emigrants to restock their provisions. Travelers "are generally well supplied with money, but by the time they get there are in want of all kinds of supplies," Bridger wrote. While he made huge profits off most travelers, he disliked penny-pinching Mormons on their way to the Salt Lake Valley. They rarely bought much, and their cattle ate the grass and scared off the big game. Bridger and Mormon leader Brigham Young feuded over many things, including operation of the trading post, Bridger's sale

LAST UNSPOILED PLACE

DOUG HOOTON, LEFT, PRESIDENT OF THE OLD
EPHRAIM MOUNTAIN MAN CLUB, HEADS A
GROUP OF LIVING HISTORY PERFORMERS WHO
RE-CREATE THE RUGGED, OUTDOOR LIFE OF
EARLY TRAPPERS AND TRADERS. ABOVE,
HOOTON AND HIS CHILDREN WARM THEM-
SELVES BY A CAMPFIRE.

of guns to Indians, jurisdiction over the sur-rounding countryside, and friction between hell-raising mountain men and pious Latter-day Saints. Young once said, "I believe that Old Bridger is death on us, and if he saw that 400,000 Indians were coming against us, and any man were to let us know, he would cut his throat."

Mormon traders outfoxed Bridger by building their own trading post 12 miles southwest of Bridger's compound. They bought Fort Bridger outright in 1855. However, the lucrative trailside business did not last. The Mormons burned the fort in 1857 rather than see it fall into the hands of Federal troops under the command of Gen. Albert Sidney Johnston. President James Buchanan had dispatched Johnston to establish Federal rule in Utah Territory, which Buchanan's administration considered to be in rebellion. The brief conflict center-ing on Utah's Mormon-dominated govern-ment and culture, including the practice of polygamy announced by Brigham Young in 1852, ended with Young's replacement as territorial governor and Buchanan's procla-mation of a blanket pardon.

The site of Fort Bridger served as a mili-tary outpost until its abandonment at the start of the Civil War. Union Pacific tracks of the transcontinental railroad bypassed the site by nine miles in 1869, sending it further into obscurity. Bridger, who had guided Johnston's troops during the so-called Utah War, pressed a claim to the fort until his death in 1881, without result.

CHAPTER 3

CHINA CAVE TO TWIN CREEK

LAST UNSPOILED PLACE

CHINA CAVE TO TWIN CREEK

Y ou might want to get in your truck, roll up the windows, and turn on the air conditioning," Darren Cox announced as he headed for a forklift and prepared to fire up his smokers.

"Bees don't like to be moved."

With that, Cox and his helper, Dave Jacobsen, both dressed head to toe in bee suits hand-sewn by Cox's wife, headed for stacks of honeybee boxes resting on pallets near a spring at the center of Cache Valley.

The setting sun cast long, fun-house shadows toward the Bear River mountains. Cox had waited until dusk on a Sunday evening in mid-June to load the bees, banking on the soporific effects of cool air and darkness to calm them.

Cox deftly maneuvered the forklift's twin prongs into the first pallet, lifted it, and swung a stack of boxes onto a small flatbed truck for transport to Bluebell Flat. The destination was a field of wildflowers and sage at an elevation of 8,700 feet in a remote corner of the Monte Cristo Mountains. Exactly where must remain a secret; Duane Cox, father of the Cox clan, prefers to keep locations and numbers of boxes under wraps in the surprisingly competitive industry.

Darren Cox piled bee boxes six deep on the flatbed. Disturbed at their jostling, the Weaver Buckfast and All American honeybees swarmed out of their homes and into the fading twilight. Their wings saturated the air with the sound of 10,000 violins warming up on the same pulsating note—overture to one of nature's oldest symphonies.

It's a golden tune to Cox, a fourth-generation beekeeper in a state whose symbol is the beehive and whose motto, "Industry," celebrates the dedication and rewards of hard work. His company, Cox Honey, rents thousands of lucrative honeybee swarms to California's almond groves from Thanksgiving until April. Almond trees won't produce nuts without bees to assist pollination from January through March; with bees, the trees yield thousands of dollars of profit per acre.

With the arrival of spring in northern Utah, when the dande-

DARREN COX, LATEST IN A LINE OF COX FAMILY BEE-KEEPERS, CHECKS HIS HIVES AT FRANKLIN BASIN. BEES AT THIS AND OTHER BEAR RIVER RANGE SITES, INCLUDING BLUEBELL FLAT, PRODUCE A SMOOTH, FLAVORFUL HONEY FROM WILDFLOWERS.

PRECEDING PAGES: WETLANDS ALONG THE LOGAN RIVER REFLECT SALMON CLOUDS AT SUNSET.

THE EXPRESSION "BUSY
AS BEES," SUCH AS THESE
HELD BY BEEKEEPER
DARREN COX
IN LOGAN CANYON,
EXPLAINS WHY HARD-
WORKING UTAH ADOPTED
THE BEEHIVE AS ITS
EMBLEM AND "INDUSTRY"
AS ITS MOTTO.

lions begin to flower, Cox retrieves his bees and prepares for the summer honey season.

Like any business, making honey has its expenses and its headaches. Healthy queen bees, necessary for strong hives, cost $16 apiece. Limiting the spread of vampire-like verroa mites, a two-decade-old plague of parasites that sucks the fluids from honeybees, requires investments in postharvest pesticides as well as constant vigilance. Mites have reduced the American beekeeping industry so thoroughly that swarms selling for $25 in the early 1990s fetched $100 or more a decade later.

"The mite is forcing us to be better beekeepers," Cox said. "It's forcing us to be more efficient."

He bought several thousand new honey frames, priced at $1.70 each, in an effort to turn simple geometry against the pests. Each frame contains hundreds of cells for storing honey and bee larvae. The new cells are narrower than those of most frames, making for a tighter squeeze. Cox figures the space will be so confining the mites won't have much room to reproduce on the bodies of the bees. In addition, replacing old, warped frames with fresh ones reduces the concentration of drone bees, which don't collect pollen.

Pyramids of new frames filled a metal barn, one of three Cox warehouses in Cache Valley, behind the Cox Honeyland store on the main Logan highway. The shop sells honey, honey butter, and fudge. The family's modern business has expanded well beyond its humble beginnings, when Darren Cox's great-grandfather worked a few hives in southern Utah at the close of the 19th century. Cox's grandfather, Marion, arrived in Cache Valley in the 1920s and shuttled his empty bee boxes by tying them onto the front and rear fenders of his bicycle. Marion eventually bought two acres in the town of Providence and sold honey out of a warehouse.

Cox's father, Duane, ran the business in the latter half of the 20th century until he moved on to a gentleman beekeeper's life of tending to his trout pond, a yard festooned with exotic plants and flowers, and the birds and bees that flock to them. Even in semiretirement, he's got honey on his mind. He tends a huge bed of orange day lilies laid out in the outline of a skep, the old-fashioned straw beehive woven in the shape of a squashed snowman. He also lectures visitors on honey's potential as a treatment for burn victims—germs don't multiply in honey because of its acidity, high sugar content, and extreme viscosity—or the benefits of eating a spoonful or two every day.

"Dad said, 'You dig your own grave with your teeth,'" Duane Cox told a visitor the day before Darren set out to move his bees to Bluebell Flat. "I tell Darren, 'Get the boxes away from the towns,'" and away from systemic pesticides and other pollutants that find their way into the food chain. Duane is also leery of vandals and unscrupulous competitors. He said that when he ran the business, he dealt with ruined boxes and poisoned bees.

"Bees, I know how they act," Duane said. "They're predictable. People are not."

Darren Cox, state director for the American Honey Producers Association, has absorbed his father's many lessons. His beehives are scattered around the pastoral countryside of northern Utah. Most produce honey from clover and alfalfa. Others lie scattered on peaks in and around Logan Canyon and produce an elixir of mountain snowberry honey.

High in the Bear River mountains, Darren Cox's bees fan out from their hives every day in storm clouds of buzzing wings. They return with heavily laden "pollen baskets," hairy leg receptacles they stuff with the male sex germ of mountain wildflowers. Flowering species near the high-altitude hives include potentilla, a shrub speckled with small yellow sunbursts; larkspur, whose spike-headed flowers range from vanilla to dark violet; hardy, yellow balsamroot, whose roots supplemented the Shoshone diet; eriogonum, whose button-shaped flowers resemble miniature strawberry tarts; and the citrus-scented leaves and snowcone blossoms of lavender-colored horsemint.

CLUSTERS OF INDIAN
PAINTBRUSH, A
SEMIPARASITIC WILD-
FLOWER, LINE THE TRAIL
FROM TONY GROVE TO
WHITE PINE LAKE.

There's also the dusty purple hound's tongue and the white-gumdrop flowers of the snowberry bush. Hound's tongue is toxic when eaten but an excellent source of pollen for honey. Michael Piep, assistant curator of the Utah State University Herbarium, calls the weedy flower "hiker's bane" because its barbs stick tightly to pants legs and more tightly to hairy hiking dogs. Snowberries, on the other hand, are edible if somewhat bitter. They helped sustain the Lewis and Clark expedition in 1805. Lewis, who first described the snowberry for science, said it was "a kind of huneysuckle which bears a white bury and rises about 4 feet high not common but to the western side of the rockey mountains."

Producing honey from mountains in an arid state involves plenty of uncertainties. There are risks from bears and fickle weather. The Cox family harvested no mountain honey crop during a half-dozen years of drought, when wildflowers barely bloomed. "The bees about starved to death by July," Darren Cox said. He fed them corn syrup to keep them alive.

In other years, a deep snowpack saturates the peaks in spring, and summer rains stimulate a flowering orgy. Mountain honeybees happily hum. Their honey is sweet, mild, and light—liquid sunshine in a jar. Darren Cox can easily distinguish it from clover honey grown in the lowlands. For that matter, he can taste the dif-

PRECEDING PAGES:
WILDFLOWERS BLOOM
NEAR TONY GROVE, HIGH
IN LOGAN CANYON.

ferences among honey from Cache Valley, Bear Lake, and Box Elder County, as well as subtle flavorings that change from year to year according to variations in temperature, terrain, sunshine, and rain. Honey, it seems, has complexities rivaling those of French wine. But then, beekeeping proved sufficient mental exercise even for the formidable Sherlock Holmes, who turned to raising the insect colonies after his retirement from detective work.

It's odd that Darren Cox would be such a honey connoisseur. Like his mother, he's allergic to bee stings. In 1983, two stings on the neck put him in the hospital. Since then, he's repeatedly tried to desensitize himself with medical treatments, but they work only for so long. The best thing to do, he said, is to get stung periodically to maintain his body's resistance.

"If I go for a year without getting stung, there's trouble," Cox said. "It's good to be stung once in a while."

"No, it's not!" said Jacobsen, preparing to help move more beehive pallets.

Cox said he's been stung as many as 50 times in one day. Asked when he was stung last, he had the answer immediately: "Saturday."

As the sun dipped behind the Wellsvilles, casting Cache Valley in shadow, Cox and Jacobsen drove toward Blacksmith Fork Canyon, south of Logan Canyon, to start the long, bumpy journey to Bluebell Flat. Near the mountains, Cox turned on his truck's headlights and hugged the curves. A dirt road off the main highway led steadily up as the last light faded in the west. Gray-green sagebrush and pale aspen trees, their trunks chalky white like ghostly sentinels in the headlights, crowded the rocky road. Deer illuminated by the high beams looked up from their browsing and bounded into the rocks; a lone coyote, more brazen, lingered in the lights before slinking into the brush.

Before the night was over, the bumps would knock out all of the truck's illumination except the headlights. It wasn't the first episode of troubles in Cox's bee truck. He remembered a notable occasion when, coming out of a canyon, a cop pulled him over while he was hauling live swarms. The officer, unaware of what awaited him, stepped out of his car and walked to the driver's window to issue a citation to Cox for having a darkened taillight and a license plate hanging by one screw. The agitated bees took careful aim at the interloper, and they fired. "He had the worst experience of his life," Cox said. Not that he wished the officer any misfortune, but bees will be bees.

It was around midnight before the bee truck reached Bluebell Flat. There, Cox and Jacobsen unloaded the boxes into a sphere of darkness so complete that no lights could be seen anywhere on the horizon. The nearest town slept about 20 miles to the southwest. Stars and planets blazed overhead. Bees beyond numbering, narcotized by the chill, awaited the warmth of dawn to set them abuzz again.

MILE MARKER 470

Cars formed a line behind a bridge construction stoplight opposite China Cave. Their occupants gawked across the Logan River at a hundred-foot cliff of gray-black dolostone, a sedimentary rock similar to limestone. A raven-haired girl on the passenger side of a white pickup truck rolled down her window, pointed, and leaned out to rest both elbows on the door's exterior. The light changed three times. The white pickup stayed immobile as cars passed on each green.

Jon and Alyson Decker, intent on sport climbing at the China Cave, did not realize they were putting on a show.

"Should I jug up and clip in, so I'm on top rope?" Alyson, working on a climb called the Secret Sharer, called down to her husband. Twenty feet below, Jon belayed his wife and shouted occasional instructions above the roar of the runoff-swollen river.

"There's big holds up there," he called. "They're all good. … Left hand up. There you go! … Now, put your foot in that pocket and drop your knee. … Nice!"

Jon has climbed hundreds of times in Logan Canyon but retains a childlike enthusiasm. He began sport climbing, in which climbers use bolts, carabiners, and nylon ropes to scale the most intimidating stone walls, when he was about ten. His brothers took him to two sites in Logan Canyon known as Fucoidal Quartzite and Second Practice Wall.

"At first I didn't like it," Jon said. "When I got to where I had to do certain handholds and footholds, and the moves got more gymnastic, I liked it better. When I had to put a foot over my head, for example, it was fun."

While attending Utah State University, Jon met Alyson and taught her to climb. They married and had two children. Their

ENTHUSIASTIC SPORT CLIMBERS JON AND ALYSON DECKER RELISH LIVING SO CLOSE TO LOGAN CANYON, WHICH IS CONSIDERED ONE OF THE PREMIER SPORT CLIMBING DESTINATIONS IN THE UNITED STATES.

elder daughter, Eden, began using ropes to make five-foot climbs when she was only three.

Alyson said she loved the sport when Jon introduced her to it. "And he was happy to have someone to come with him, so it worked out pretty good," she said. Jon had other climbing buddies, "but I guess I was cuter."

When not climbing, Jon markets orthopedic implants. He's never had to make use of his own products; his worst fall resulted only in a bruised tailbone. While the sport climbs he makes in Logan Canyon look dangerous, they result in fewer injuries than skiing, horseback riding, or motocross. Climbers wear harnesses

JON DECKER WORKS HIS WAY ACROSS THE WALL OF CHINA CAVE, A ROCK FACE FEATURING SOME OF THE TOUGHEST SPORTS CLIMBS IN THE WORLD, WITH THE BELAYING HELP OF HIS WIFE.

fitted with nylon ropes. Their ascents follow routes in the rock fitted with bolts strong enough to support the weight of a car.
Careful climbers still fall when their forearms give out, but their
bodies drop only the length between bolts.

Climbing guidebooks proclaim Logan Canyon as one of the
meccas of sport climbing, along with Smith Rock in Oregon; Rifle,
Colorado; Lander, Wyoming; and American Fork, at the southern
end of Utah's Wasatch Front.

Logan Canyon is renowned for rock formations that resist chip-
ping, offer a variety of challenges, have spectacular views, and are

SPORT CLIMBER JON
DECKER HANGS ABOVE
THE LOGAN RIVER,
WHICH FORMED CHINA
CAVE BY CUTTING INTO
THE BASE OF A TOWER-
ING WALL OF ROCK.

within an easy hike of the highway. The first to successfully climb
a route without hanging from a rope wins the right to name it.
Climbers have created names such as Slugfest, Yellow Pages, Crag in
the Sky, Praise the Lowered, and Crotch Shot.

China Cave, so named because of it being part of the same
sedimentary formations in Logan Canyon that gave rise to the
China Wall, has some of the toughest routes on Earth, according
to the Yosemite Decimal System. It assigns numbers from 1 to 5
to climbs based on difficulty. Anything starting with a 5 requires
a rope. The toughest climbs get numbers such as 5.9 and 5.10,

up to the expert designations from 5.12 through 5.15. Super Tweak at the China Cave, designated the first 5.14b in America, has been climbed fewer than ten times, Jon Decker said. He added a crucial distinction: Those who make it to the top of a route without ever hanging on their rope can say they've "done" or "climbed" it. Those who needed their ropes can only claim, "I've been on it."

The slope is the most difficult part of China Cave, which is situated across the highway from the entrance to Right Hand Fork and up the canyon from the most distinct layers of the China Wall. Climbers must hang on a rock that leans over an open space cut by the river. That's the so-called "cave" where horse-drawn wagons rested out of the sun before the road was paved. Jon said it's hard to hang parallel to the rock face when the weight of one's midsection pulls straight down. The best climbers have the body fat of a coat hanger and steel cables for forearms, enabling them to support themselves with just their fingertips. Popeye the Sailor Man had the perfect body for a rock climber.

Decker, at five foot nine and 150 pounds, said he felt a little out of shape after not climbing for a while. Nevertheless, he went up Crimpfest, christened for its tiny fingerholds, and a route at "385," a long-gone mile marker near the Jardine Juniper Trailhead at Wood Camp. His favorite route is Crag in the Sky, a half-hour hike from the highway, because its height commands a view of the entire lower canyon.

"You can tell the good routes by all of the white chalk marks on the rock," Jon said. Climbers discern the direction of the best handholds by reading the rock. If there's a lot of chalk on the right side of a hole, the handhold is on the left. Little white tick marks indicate the toes of climbing shoes. A well-traveled rock, spattered with chalk, appears to suffer from leprosy.

Typical climbs last only five to fifteen minutes.

"So tired," Jon said after Alyson lowered him from the top of a climb. His forearms throbbed from exertion. He removed his climbing shoes before reaching the floor of China Cave, then jumped with a splash into mud and water.

"One move was so fun, I thought I was going to torque my back," he said.

MILE MARKER 471

Through a green corridor of trees above China Cave, the Logan River and U.S. 89 make a sharp bend to the right, curving around a site named Wood Camp in memory of the lumber station the Mormon Church established there in the 19th century. A gravel

road north of the river leads to the start of the five-mile ascent to the Jardine Juniper. The single-track trail rises from 5,400 feet at the trailhead to 7,200 feet at the top, where a ridge affords spectacular views of mountains to the east and west. Horseback riders and mountain bikers flock to the trail in the summer, while hunters and cross-country skiers visit in the cooler months.

The trail starts in sun-bathed fields of sage before a series of switchbacks passes through fir, juniper, and enormous quaking aspens measuring up to 16 inches in diameter. In early summer, a keen observer can count dozens of species of wildflowers along the trail, including Indian paintbrush, lupine, mule's ear, scarlet gilia, and, in the duff beneath the evergreens, striped coralroot. The bloodred and magenta coralroot, a member of the orchid family, lacks chlorophyll and thus the ability to make its own food. It survives as a parasite, taking nourishment from fungus underground. Once the coralroot plant blooms, it may go dormant for years before flowering again.

The switchbacks on the way to the summit contain small marine fossils. Most common are brachiopods. Seen in cross section in the dolostone, they form white arcs in the darker rock. More fossils lie below Mount Elmer, which stays snow-tipped well into summer. After rounding the last switchback, hikers can see the 9,676-foot

TREE BRANCHES MEET ABOVE U.S. 89 NEAR CHINA CAVE, FORMING A GREEN AND LEAFY TUNNEL.

PRECEDING PAGES:
THE JARDINE JUNIPER,
A UTAH LANDMARK,
TOWERS ABOVE LOGAN
CANYON AT THE END OF A
DELIGHTFUL TRAIL.

TIGER SWALLOWTAIL
BUTTERFLIES SUCK MOIS-
TURE FROM LOGAN RIVER
MUD NEAR WOOD CAMP,
TRAILHEAD OF THE HIKE
TO THE JARDINE JUNIPER.

mountain at the head of Cottonwood Canyon. At its base, the talus contains horn corals from when the Bear River mountains lay at the bottom of a tropical sea.

At the top of the trail, the path splits. The right-hand trail stays in the sun, providing open views of mountain slopes where land-slides have carved treeless vertical paths like ski runs. The left-hand trail dips into an aspen-coniferous forest, where the shady ground gives rise to woodland strawberries and cow parsnips. After the trails meet on the east side of the ridge, completing a circle, they drop 300 feet to the Jardine Juniper.

Hikers have been making pilgrimages to the giant Rocky Mountain juniper since Maurice Linford discovered it during a walk in fall 1923. He snapped a photograph of the tree, developed it, and shared it with the botany department at Utah State Agricultural College. "At once it was realized that that tree was a very extraordinary tree and as soon as the snow was off the follow-ing spring an excursion was made to it," Professor George Hill wrote in August 1925. "Every student in Botany since that time has

been to the tree on one or more occasion." The tree was named in honor of U.S. Secretary of Agriculture William Jardine, who previously taught at the university in Logan. The juniper measures nearly 27 feet around and 45 feet high.

At the time, tree experts proclaimed the juniper to be 3,200 years old. Revised estimates now place the age closer to 1,500 years. Either way, the tree inspires awe. "The old tree has so fortified itself that it has become a tower of strength," Hill wrote. "It is gradually breaking the cliff where it is growing, asunder, and if one views the tree from the south one can see that it is pushing, slowly pushing off several tons of rocky material." Only its highest branches remain green.

MILE MARKER 472

A Sunday in June, 8:30 a.m. Air temperature, 66 degrees Fahrenheit. Water temperature, 43 degrees. Volume of water in the Logan River, 843 cubic feet per second.

Negatives: Potential for collisions at 15 miles an hour with boulders the size of Humvees; broken bones, scrapes, hypothermia, and—lest anyone forget—drowning.

Positives: Incredible scenery and an addictive adrenaline rush.

"*Woo-hoooo!*" yelled kayaker Josh Anderson as he spun like a spiraling football in the whitewater above Wood Camp.

His goal each year is to hit the water at least 150 days, most of them on the Logan River. It was easier before he began working in landscaping and for Common Ground Outdoor Adventures, a Logan-based organization that introduces people with mental, physical, and emotional disabilities to rafting, canoeing, hiking, mountain biking, fishing and other activities in and around Logan Canyon. Anderson's continued studies in special education at Utah State University also eat into his kayaking time. Nevertheless, he rates kayaking whitewater as a priority somewhere below his marriage and somewhere above everything else.

While much of Cache Valley spent Sunday morning in church, Anderson and his friend Wally Macfarlane, a Salt Lake City mapmaker, decided to worship at the shrine of nature. They tossed their hard-plastic kayaks into the back of a red pickup truck and drove to a giant boulder they called the "Monolith," above Wood Camp.

Anderson removed his black shorts, sandals, and black baseball cap. He took off his short-sleeved print shirt to reveal a well-tanned and muscled chest, ornamented with a ring in each nipple. He slipped into his "dry top," an elaborate torso-hugging suit equipped with latex gaskets to keep water away from his skin. He then stepped into a black spray skirt and worked it slowly over his

PRECEDING PAGES:
RIPARIAN VEGETATION,
ORANGE IN EARLY
AUTUMN, COLORS
COTTONWOOD
CANYON, A FINGER OF
LOGAN CANYON.

WALLY MACFARLANE
CARRIES HIS KAYAK
ALONG THE EDGE OF
U.S. 89, WHICH ALLOWS
EASY RIVER ACCESS
THROUGH NEARLY ALL
OF LOGAN CANYON.

hips. "Must have gained weight," he grunted. The skirt looked like an old-fashioned blacksmith's apron with an extra flap in the back. Its edge contained an elastic band to fit around the opening in the kayak, making an air-bubble seal around the legs. The final touches to Anderson's whitewater wardrobe were a lifejacket, a helmet, and special shoes. He held off putting on his noseplug until just before beginning his run.

Anderson and Macfarlane put in above the Monolith near a patch of elderberry bushes. They slipped into the current and paddled ferociously, left-right-left-right-right-right, to maintain control. Under ideal conditions, a kayaker can ride a breaking wave in midstream for minutes at a time. Anderson called the move "hanging out." Afterward, the kayaker can release and go downstream; "eddy out" to a calm patch of water; or lose control and let the river dictate the next move.

"It's kinda trashy, man. Just hang on!" Anderson, riding the break, called to Macfarlane. He held steady for a few seconds at a 60-degree angle, his right arm buried to the elbow in the foam. The current then flipped sideways. His head emerged upright seconds later, hair and beard soaked by the icy water. *"Woo-hoo!"* he hollered.

After getting out of the river, Anderson said the scariest moments occur when the water flips a paddler head down and pushes the kayak into a rock. To get out, the kayaker may have to pop the spray skirt and kick free. He's grateful he hasn't had to take that test; on his ledger the fun of kayaking has greatly outweighed any bad experiences. Anderson likened the rush of whitewater to a bear dancing in the spring upon its emergence from hibernation.

Macfarlane's turn. The bigger man paddled to a white ridge in midstream and turned to face the current. He rode the wave for several seconds like a sitting surfer, his arms working madly with the paddle.

"Oh, he's blown it," Anderson said. Sure enough, two seconds later

Macfarlane "flushed," rocketing downstream with the current. How did Anderson know? "When the bow dives underwater, he slows relative to the current. Like surfing." The increase in resistance gives the current more power to push against the kayak, and down it goes.

WALLY MACFARLANE SURFS ON A WAVE NEAR THE MONOLITH, A GIANT BOULDER IN THE MIDDLE OF THE LOGAN RIVER.

VOLUNTEERS AND WORK-
ERS ASSIGNED BY THE
MORMON CHURCH KEPT
TEMPLE FORK SAWMILL
BUSY BETWEEN 1877 AND
1884. THE MILL SUPPLIED
LUMBER FOR THE LOGAN
TEMPLE AND A NETWORK
OF RAILROAD LINES.

Anderson grew up in Texas and Wyoming before moving to Cache Valley in 2003. He usually starts his kayaking season in February on the runs of southern Utah and southern Idaho. Running the Logan River starts around April, depending on the water level and temperature.

The canyon holds many charms for the kayaker. First, it's close to school. Anderson can knock out a 15-minute run over the lunch hour and be back to the USU campus in time for afternoon classes. Second, it has a variety of runs, including the potential for a trip stretching from the river's upper reaches in Franklin Basin through midtown Logan, more than 30 miles away. Third, the highway through the canyon has frequent pullouts, allowing easy access to the river. And finally, portions of the Logan River rate among the toughest challenges. The "Staircase," near the mouth of the canyon, can be conquered only by the elite. The run through a narrow channel is dotted with boulder after boulder, like studs on a dog collar.

"To have that quality of whitewater five minutes from the house is pretty cool," Anderson said. He intends to keep coming back.

MILE MARKER 476

When the Mormon pioneers ventured into Logan Canyon in the late 1850s, they found it heavily timbered with lodgepole pines and a variety of fir known as red pine. The Mormons had big plans for developing Cache Valley, and the timber seemed ideal for construction. Trouble was, they didn't know how to get the wood out of the rugged canyon. In 1860, three men struggled up the rocky crease along the Logan River and cut the first logs. They rolled them into the river and tried to float them into the valley. The whitewater and boulders turned the logs to kindling, forcing the would-be lumberjacks to move to the more accessible Green Canyon to the north.

Eventually, roads pushed into Logan Canyon, and by the early 1870s five sawmills were busily cutting trees. They not only supplied the building needs in town but also the railroad ties for new lines fanning out from the newly completed transcontinental line. The United Order Manufacturing and Building Company of Logan, a Mormon cooperative, cut 53,000 ties in 1875 alone, to help build the Oregon Short Line. As a single tree yielded only two to three ties, the cutting took a heavy toll on the canyon's forests. During construction of the Utah and Northern Railroad a short time later, virtually any tree that could supply a tie felt the woodsman's ax.

The railroads' appetite for lumber led to competition to secure the best stands of trees. Coe and Carter, a company that supplied railroads with crossties, scouted Logan Canyon for untapped stands of fir. Discovering that a rival had its designs on the canyon, the Church of Jesus Christ of Latter-day Saints hurried its own team into a richly timbered side canyon known as Maughan's Fork. "When the Coe and Carter outfit arrived some forty-eight hours later," wrote historian Marion Everton, "they found the first logs laid out for a big sawmill and men busily engaged in constructing shelters but not too busy to tell visitors that they intended to continue the occupation of Maughan's Fork with the exclusion of any and all other outfits."

FOLLOWING PAGES: SCARLET GILIA, A MEMBER OF THE PHLOX FAMILY, BLOOMS ALONGSIDE RUSHING WATERS THAT ONCE POWERED THE TEMPLE FORK SAWMILL.

LOGAN'S SLITHERING DENIZENS

Every Eden has its serpents. Logan Canyon's species pose little threat to most humans, although some cause double takes.

"We have them brought in occasionally because people think they have two heads," Utah State University biology professor Edmund Brodie, Jr., said of northern Utah's rubber boas. "The tail looks very much like the head."

The tails of the one- to two-foot, dull-brown snakes usually bear teeth marks from mice, as well as telltale compression of vertebrae. That's because the rubber boa typically slides into a mouse nest to feed, fending off the angry mother by jabbing its tail like a spear or club while its business end keeps busy swallowing the young.

Around humans, however, the rubber boa never bites. If you pick it up, it will calmly coil in your hand or wrap around your forearm, Brodie said.

Logan Canyon also is home to one venomous species, the western rattlesnake. Its scientific name, *Crotalus viridis,* comes from *crotalon,* a Greek word meaning "little bell," which refers to its rattle, and the Latin for green. The canyon's variety isn't green, however; it's marked by dark blotches against a tan or gray background. The western rattlesnake's toxin is too weak and its size too small—rarely reaching 30 inches, compared with, say, the 5-foot Eastern diamondbacks of the southeastern lowlands—to cause much worry for adult humans, although pets and children are at some risk. Mostly, western rattlesnakes and people live with mutual respect and nonaggression. Like most

WHEN THREATENED, THE NONVENOMOUS GOPHER SNAKE WILL APE A RATTLER.

snakes, western rattlers don't pick fights. "You'll walk by a lot of snakes in the area, and you'll never see them," Brodie said. "Step over them, and they don't move."

Not so, all too often, with the canyon's gopher snakes, also known as bull snakes. As a defense mechanism when threatened, the gopher snake mimics an angry rattler in appearance and sound. It displays a splotchy pattern much like the western rattler's; its tail vibrates in dry leaves to imitate the rattle's tattletale buzz; and it hisses, puffs its body, and strikes vigorously to intimidate intruders. At five to six feet long, the gopher snake scares a lot of people who can't distinguish it from the rattler. Brodie said a friend once called him to say he had caught a rattlesnake and trapped it in a can. "I went over, looked in the can, and reached in and grabbed it," Brodie recalled. "He said, *'Nooo!'"*

Brodie smiled. "It was a bull snake."

The mill sawed its first board in November 1877. As the Mormons used the wood to build Logan's temple, the side canyon soon received a new name: Temple Fork. The canyon, five miles above Wood Camp, opens from a narrow entrance at the Logan River to an expanse of rolling hills and fields. The sawmill operated a few miles up a bubbling stream. Workers at the sawmill found more than enough trees to supply the temple's needs and began supplying surplus wood to the Utah and Northern.

The Mormon Church couldn't completely rely on volunteer labor during the summer, when most Cache Valley men worked their farms. Individual wards of the Church assigned men to work either on the sawmill or the temple itself, two blocks east of the tabernacle in downtown Logan.

The sawmill work offered steady labor. Some 20 to 30 men cut trees, ran the saw, and hauled lumber to the temple. At least one woman worked at Temple Fork. A pregnant teenager, Cynthia Nielson Wight, cooked meals at the sawmill while her husband acted as a foreman. "I earned $70.00 which I spent in buying things to keep house after paying my tithing," she wrote.

It wasn't all work. Mill workers observed Sunday religious services and celebrated holidays. The sawmill superintendent once stumbled onto a scene of his masculine work crew performing a square dance, with some of the men wearing a bow on the arm to designate them as "female" dancing partners. "Anyone who failed to enter into the fun was liable to be seized by a big foreman and pulled onto the floor," historian Paige Lewis wrote.

The church closed the mill in 1884 and tried to find a buyer. None came forward; the railroads had moved so far north they could draw on closer supplies in Montana. The abandoned mill burned under mysterious circumstances in the winter of 1886. Two sets of footprints in the snow led to and from the ashes. Indications pointed to arson, but nobody ever stood trial.

The Temple Sawmill was never rebuilt. Its lasting monuments, besides the Logan Temple and a web of railroad tracks, could be found in the mounds of sawdust left behind. Cleanup crews removed piles of dust more than 20 feet high in the early 1970s to make the site lush and green once again. Today, reaching the Temple Sawmill site requires a short, easy hike along the Temple Fork. The glade is covered with larkspur and mule's-ear flowers in the spring. Creek water splashes out of a narrow vale. And all around, the children and grandchildren of trees once cut in the name of commerce and religion have grown tall.

A MEETING OF THE RAILS

As soon as Meriwether Lewis and William Clark returned to Washington in 1806 with the news that no all-water route existed to the Pacific Ocean, Americans began dreaming of other ways to unite East and West. The prospects looked bleak. The Rocky Mountains obliterated the possibility of canals, which had fed the engines of the Eastern economy, and the rugged, dry wilderness west of the 100th meridian seemed more of a barrier than a highway to the promised land. Newspaper publisher Horace Greeley, who passed through in 1859, believed the West so barren and dusty that settlement would require at least a century.

The railroad changed that. It was a bold move in 1862, during the darkest days of the Civil War, when President Abraham Lincoln signed the Pacific Railroad Act to construct a rail line spanning the continent. The plan called for the Union Pacific Railroad to head west from Council Bluffs, Iowa, and the Central Pacific Railroad to lay track east from Sacramento, California, with the two sides meeting somewhere in the trackless West. The Civil War delayed work

CHINESE LABORERS CROWD CAMP VICTORY, SO NAMED BECAUSE CENTRAL PACIFIC CREWS KNEW THE TRANSCONTINENTAL LINE SOON WOULD BE COMPLETED NEARBY.

on the line, but by 1868 the Union Pacific tracks reached Utah Territory.

Popular history holds that Chinese laborers laid the track from the West, and Irish immigrants did the same from the East. In Utah, however, the Mormons constructed much of the transcontinental line. Utah's church leaders won $2 million in contracts from the Union Pacific to do all of the work on a 150-mile stretch of track, including grading, tie-laying, bridging, and tunneling. The Central Pacific granted smaller contracts. It

CENTRAL PACIFIC RAILROAD CONSTRUCTION WORKERS CROSS A TRESTLE ON FLATCARS NEAR PROMONTORY POINT, ABOVE. OPPOSITE BOTTOM, THE GAP THAT SEPARATED EAST AND WEST NARROWED TO A SINGLE RAIL'S LENGTH, THEN CLOSED WITH THE CEREMONI-AL DRIVING OF THE GOLDEN SPIKE, OPPOSITE TOP, ON MAY 10, 1869.

seemed like a sweet deal for the Latter-day Saints, who would get the benefit not only of the railroads' cash, but also of the instant

access to markets for local food and timber. Mormons from Cache Valley not only helped build the railroad but also pocketed money from wheat, butter, and eggs they sold to the work crews.

It came as a shock in May 1869 when the Central Pacific and Union Pacific failed to pay all their debts after the golden spike united their two lines at Promontory, just north of the Great Salt Lake. Mormon leader Brigham Young settled for what he could get: railroad equipment valued at $600,000, with which Utah built a connecting line between Salt Lake City and the transcontinental rails at Ogden.

Dry, empty, and remote, Promontory Summit became the site of the union of two railroads because of congressional intervention. The two competing railroads received grants of rights-of-way and subsidies for each mile of track they laid. Greedy grading crews passed each in the race to gobble up as much land as possible, creating at least 225 miles of parallel track stretching from Ogden to Humboldt Wells, Nevada. Congress put an end to the madness by ordering the railroads to meet "at or near Ogden." The final route made the town of Corinne, the northernmost point on the line and a source of good water, the logical jumping-off point for new tracks to connect to gold and silver mines in Montana.

Corinne, east of Promontory, boomed as a lusty, gambling, hard-drinking, non-Mormon town unlike anything Utah Territory had ever seen. Local legend has it that Brigham Young stood in the bed of a buckboard wagon near Corinne and cursed the town to the depths of hell. But it was Mother Nature and human enterprise, not fire and brimstone, that shattered Corinne. Farmers found the soil too alkaline for most crops, and the 1878 completion of a new terminus for the Utah and Northern Railroad in Blackfoot, Idaho, drained much of the commerce. The final blow came in 1904, when a direct line across the Great Salt Lake isolated the town. Corinne became the sleepy hamlet that it still remains. Some of the original railroad workers who finished their work north of the Great Salt Lake decided to stay in Utah. Up to 300 Chinese lived in Corinne during its boomtown days, and small Chinatowns blossomed in Ogden, Park City, and Salt Lake City.

Railroad lines inched north from the Wasatch Front and reached Logan in 1873. The train's small engine huffed under the strain of the free rides offered to Logan res-

idents, forcing the passengers to get off and push to and from the Logan River. More powerful engines arrived the next year.

Rail lines absorbed the lumber harvested in Logan Canyon and shipped the sheep and cattle fattened on the canyon's slopes to markets outside Cache Valley. However, the benefits of easy connections to the outside world were balanced by challenges. No longer could the Mormons, who had fled

LAST UNSPOILED PLACE

persecution in the East, rely on the mountains to isolate them from outsiders. Gentiles (non-Mormons) arrived along with their alcohol, gambling, and coffee, all frowned upon by devout members of

NO. 5 OF THE UTAH-IDAHO CENTRAL RAILROAD PAUSES IN LOGAN IN THE EARLY 20TH CENTURY. TRAINS ENDED NORTHERN UTAH'S ISOLATION.

Young's church. They brought their own businesses to compete with the local enterprises, and they brought their own religious ideas, too. It's no wonder that in 1869 the *Deseret News,* the Mormon daily newspaper of Salt Lake City, called the completion of the transcontinental railroad "of more significance and interest" to Utah residents than "to any other portion of their fellow citizens of the Union."

CHAPTER 4

TWIN CREEK TO FRANKLIN BASIN

LAST UNSPOILED PLACE

TWIN CREEK TO FRANKLIN BASIN

Fear teaches. Fear inspires. When conquered, fear builds self-esteem, leadership, and trust.

In a controlled environment, a little fear is good. That's a key message learned on the Ropes Course, run by the Conference Services office at Utah State University.

Without fear, where would participants in one of the most unusual attractions associated with Logan Canyon find the motivation to test their limits and discover the value of teamwork? In harness and helmet, high in the air, they grasp a fundamental lesson. You wanna get down? Talk to each other.

For years the Ropes Course brought organizations, companies, church groups, and athletic teams to the green slopes near Tony Grove, high in Logan Canyon. Then that course closed and a new one looking much the same opened in a field opposite the canyon mouth. The new course attracted scores of university students taking advantage of the nearby physical, mental, and emotional challenges. Plans call for the course to return someday soon to the high country, near Beaver Mountain, and become part of a more fully developed motivational center. Interest in ropes courses is booming nationwide, and the USU operation is booked most days in the summer although its only advertising is by word of mouth.

"A ropes course is hard to explain," said Chelsea Nelson, the course manager and a student at USU. "People who come are looking to unify a group and to work on leadership skills, but every group wants to emphasize different things. Youth groups come, and they want to emphasize self-esteem, for example."

Stations have names such as Acid Pit, Partner Triangle, Alligator Swamp, Zigzag, and Wobbly Log. One station, the Perch, consists of a high pole studded with knobs and topped with a plate. The goal is to climb the pole, stand on the plate, and jump laterally—while safely harnessed to a rope—to grab a ring hanging in space. Some people do just that. Others may find merely climbing partway up the pole to be one of the biggest challenges of their lives. Both results are OK, Nelson said. The point is to learn and to grow, individually and collectively.

MEMBERS OF A LOGAN WARD OF THE LDS CHURCH TEST THEMSELVES ON THE ROPES COURSE. THE COURSE BEGAN OPERATIONS NEAR TONY GROVE, MOVED TO THE MOUTH OF LOGAN CANYON, AND IS EXPECTED TO RETURN TO THE HIGH COUNTRY.

PRECEDING PAGES: PUMPKINS LIE READY FOR HARVEST IN THE FROSTY FIELDS OF CACHE VALLEY.

"If people have poor communication skills, we are able to see that. People are afraid to ask their belayer for help, and we focus on that. 'What do you need right now? Do you need more tension? Do you need people to be quiet?' So we focus on why it's important to tell the people around you what you need."

Another exercise puts 40 blindfolded people on the grass and hands them a single rope. Instructors ask the group to fashion the rope into a perfect square.

GAS-POWERED SNOW-
MOBILES CARVE TRAILS
AMONG THE SLOPES OF
THE BEAR RIVER RANGE.
USU STUDENTS ARE
LEADING THE DEVELOP-
MENT OF AN EFFICIENT,
ALL-ELECTRIC VERSION.

"And they try," Nelson said. "We talk about the difference between a rectangle and a square. If there are 40 people in a group, there are 40 different ideas on how to make a square. And then when they get close, they say, 'It's good enough.' Afterward, we say, 'If your bosses want a square, and you give them a rectangle, is that good enough?' Or with an athletic team, if the coach wants Play No. 1, and you do Play No. 2, is that good enough?"

One bright morning in May, teams of a half dozen or so from a software company and an eating disorder treatment center visited the Ropes Course. Their first assignment: Mohawk Walk. A facilitator asked them to pretend they had survived an earthquake but were stuck on top of a burning building. Cables hung between the rooftops, and the participants had to flee to safety by walking across the ropes. If they fell, they died. In reality, the ropes were stretched only a short hop off the ground between a set of wooden poles. Nevertheless, the intensity was real. Participants quickly learned that nobody could succeed alone; the ropes' arrangement required everyone to figure out how to push and pull to steady each other as they crossed. As they clung to each other and made the ropes shake with a frantic palsy, they shouted encouragement and, at the facilitators' request, avoided negative words.

Nine-year-old Alec Peterson got his reward on the Zip Line, a cable linking the top of a high tower with a shorter pole far away. Alec donned his harness and helmet, climbed the tower, and slid a hundred yards across the compound.

A SNOWMOBILER ZIPS ALONG A PORTION OF THE MORE THAN 300 MILES OF GROOMED TRAILS IN THE BEAR RIVER RANGE.

LAST UNSPOILED PLACE

"Nice job!" shouted Jamie Justice, who had helped him get ready for the slide. "Were you scared?"

"Yep," said Alec.

"Good."

MILE MARKER 479

Fat flakes fell as the evening sky dissolved into violet.

Far from the city, high in snowy mountain country, surrounded by silent space filling up with white as the temperature dropped and the light failed—not exactly ideal conditions for most travelers, but nearly perfect to test a radically new type of snowmobile.

Utah State University engineering student Nathan Hansen and his friends got to work. They unloaded their prototype and pushed it onto the packed powder of the access road connecting U.S. 89 with Tony Grove, a mountain lake surrounded by evergreens. They opened the hood and made some last-minute adjustments. Then Hansen slung his leg over the seat, settled himself, and turned the key.

If this was the start of a revolution in winter transportation, Hansen and his team had just fired the first shot.

Silently.

The 12-member student engineering team had built an all-electric, zero-emission snowmobile from scratch, using donated parts and whatever they could afford to buy, "literally, out of the change dish," Hansen said. Yellowstone National Park, interested in the development of a gas-free, silent snowmobile for use in the pristine wilderness, had donated a nine-year-old black chassis. An outlay of $500 had bought a set of ten, 12-volt boat batteries, weighing a total of 380 pounds, for the power source. The team had installed a cylindrical motor and configured a direct-drive transmission, similar to a timing belt, to improve engine efficiency. Suspension had been beefed up to support the batteries stashed in a row beneath the driver's seat.

"Relative to gas [snowmobiles], ours is significantly heavier," Hansen said. "There are better battery technologies out there. They're just much more expensive on this kind of scale. If we had the money to get some lithium polymer batteries, we would easily double our range. And we'd have quadruple the charge density."

Nevertheless, boat batteries have advantages. They're easy to find and easy to charge. A wall outlet and a few hours restore them to life.

Like many engineers, Hansen comfortably peppered his conversation with phrases such as charge density, torque curve, and

concept viability. Yet more than a speck of little-kid enthusiasm enlivened the engineering team's behavior when the snowmobile, which team member Ron Silver had dubbed Snow Watt, zoomed along the access road.

"Look at the rooster tail!" someone crowed when Snow Watt kicked up a question-mark-shaped fountain of powder during initial acceleration.

The snowmobile sped up the hill in a long, straight line. A low whine, barely audible from ten yards away, emerged from the treads. With Hansen at the controls, Snow Watt disappeared over a low ridge a hundred yards from his team members.

They waited for him to return.

They waited some more.

Finally, curious, they hiked over the rise. There was Hansen,

SKIERS' LANTERNS LIGHT
A YURT HIGH IN THE
BACKCOUNTRY IN A
LONG-EXPOSURE
PHOTOGRAPH.

stuck in three feet of soft powder at the side of the trail. Snow Watt had buried its nose as Hansen tried to execute a tight "U" for his return to the bottom of the road.

"Well, it won't do what it wasn't designed to do," Hansen announced. He seemed strangely happy, explaining that he intended to "abuse" the machine by pushing it to its limits, and perhaps a bit beyond. Such punishment is essential to preparing for a competition, he explained. He found that Snow Watt would not cut through deep drifts during a sharp turn, but that was no surprise. It had been designed to travel up to 10 miles, at 20 miles an hour, along a trail or slope. That kind of mission might prove useful in wilderness areas where noisy, gas-powered snowmobiles frighten wildlife and spew pollutants. Rangers might use electric sleds in patrols and rescue operations, changing mounts at recharging stations like Pony Express riders along the frontier. The sleds also could be used to groom a trail system or take riders on short commutes. And scientists might employ them during data-gathering expeditions to remote glaciers, in order to prevent exhaust gases from contaminating samples of ancient ice and the air pockets they contain.

The National Science Foundation is pushing for development of just such a machine for use at the Summit Research Station in Greenland. Months before the Tony Grove test, NSF scientists contacted Hansen after finding his name on a Web search for electric snowmobile designers. The foundation asked him to submit a proposal for funding. It wanted something nobody had come close to building: a zero-emission machine that could go 10 miles, at 20 miles an hour, and pull a 1,000-pound trailer. At the time, Hansen's best run ended at three miles; he didn't even know if the NSF's performance criteria were possible, given the existing technology. Naturally, he felt a bit uncomfortable submitting a fixed-cost proposal to a huge federal agency to create a state-of-the-art machine without being able to visualize the steps to build it. Instead, he and his father turned in an alternative proposal, after the submission deadline, aimed at a more investigative approach to technological development. The NSF passed it over, Hansen said, and pursued discussions about development with McGill University in Montreal, Canada.

Hansen took his plan to Utah State University and oversaw the creation of a snowmobile marrying acceptable performance and low cost. The result, Snow Watt, faced a do-or-die date in March 2006 at a collegiate design competition sponsored by the Society of Automotive Engineers. The Clean Snowmobile Challenge in Houghton, Michigan, would test college students' redesigned electric and gas-powered snowmobiles. The trial at Tony Grove aimed to eliminate the bugs before the competition.

"Our snowmobile is clean and quiet and could really help cut down on air and noise pollution in areas where snowmobile use is common, especially for utilitarian purposes," Hansen said. "Our snowmobile could easily get around a snowy town in Michigan."

Hansen's motivations extended beyond making an environmentally friendly machine. Production of a zero-emission snowmobile would earn him senior-level design credits from the USU College of Engineering. A successful test would help fulfill his graduation requirements.

Hansen, a broad-shouldered, dark-haired student with an impressive pair of Elvis sideburns, began his work on electric snowmobiles after taking cross-country ski trips into the mountains near his home in Midway, Utah, southeast of Salt Lake City. "You can hear snowmobilers a mile up the canyon," he said, "and you can smell them five minutes after they pass you. I said, 'There's got to be a better way.'"

Although he's not a snowmobile fanatic, he took on production as an engineering problem worthy of solution. Hansen's father, also an engineer, helped him build early models. Their first attempt worked, but just barely. Hansen called it "a gutless wonder." A revised version traveled about one mile, at ten miles an

WADING INTO TONY
GROVE LAKE CAN RAISE
GOOSE BUMPS EVEN IN
JUNE AND JULY, WHEN
TRACES OF SNOW LURK
IN THE SHADOWS OF
EVERGREENS ALONG THE
SOUTH SHORE.

hour. After that, Hansen and his dad built an electric snowmobile in their garage that would go three times as far, and much faster. They hauled that version to Yellowstone, resulting in the donation of the chassis.

The USU team members took that chassis and pushed the design envelope. Their ultimate goal, somewhere in the future, is to produce a snowmobile that can run at least 40 miles on one charge, and then recharge easily in a few hours. They face a major hurdle in the chicken-or-egg problem of fund-raising: To attract money to develop technology, they need to demonstrate the potential of that technology. Their most daunting engineering challenge remains extending the electric snowmobile's radius of operation. With a range of ten miles or so, the snowmobile might find a niche as a utility vehicle. Performing significantly beyond that range would open doors to the big money of the outdoor recreation market.

Snow Watt's performance in Michigan would be one small, early step of that long journey.

Hansen and friends put their machine through its paces at Tony Grove until night grew too dark to continue. Then they hauled it back to their USU lab for late-night tinkering. Hansen promised to talk more about Snow Watt after returning from Michigan, and he was as good as his word.

"Our snowmobile was the highest performance electric snowmobile that this competition (or anyone for that matter) has ever seen, and we performed better than anyone expected us to," Hansen said as summer began to melt Logan Canyon's snow.

The USU team dominated the electric snowmobile category, winning first place. Honors included best zero-emissions design and range, as well as the competition's rookie of the year award. Snow Watt traveled 9.5 miles, which was 2 miles farther than any other electric snowmobile. It even ran effectively against gas-powered snowmobiles.

Snow Watt passed an even greater test in summer 2006. Hansen's team loaned Snow Watt to the NSF for its summer use on the glaciers of Greenland. It goes "pretty darn close" to 10 miles at 20 miles an hour, Hansen said, and pulls more than 1,000 pounds on a trailer. Utah State University and McGill delivered rival machines to the Greenland station in May. McGill's broke down within a month and was sent home. Snow Watt kept right on running.

The USU team planned to return to the Clean Snowmobile Challenge in 2007, Hansen said, to continue to build a case for electric snowmobiles. Their machine, Snow Watt, had set the

TWIN CREEK TO FRANKLIN BASIN

standard for performance, and he was certain Utah State would exceed it in years to come.

MILE MARKER 480

At first, the cavers from the Bear River Grotto caving association thought they had found Lucifer's Lair in summer 2000. Accounts in old caving journals had pegged the lair as being about 300 feet deep, and that seemed to match the depth of the cave's entrance pit. But something was amiss. At the bottom of the pit, high above the lake at Tony Grove, a giant snow cone towered above the rubble. The ice stood dozens of feet high and looked like a mound of swirled, soft ice cream fit for Paul Bunyan.

"I looked around, and the walls in the cavern were really covered with ice," said Idaho caver Vern Bowden, who explored the pit that summer with Thomas Haskett. "And as we were in there, a big piece of ice fell off the wall. So we got on the rope and came out."

Further study revealed the cave couldn't be Lucifer's Lair. The cave Haskett and Bowden were looking for had huge boulders on the floor instead of a snowy pyramid. Lucifer's Lair also dropped, after an initial squeeze, into large chambers dubbed Outer Darkness and Forbidden Treasures. The new cave seemed to have no big rooms off the entrance. So Bowden and Haskett named the cave Deception Pit, "because we'd been deceived," Bowden said.

And Deception Pit it remained until cave explorer Ryan Shurtz of Clearfield, Utah, stepped inside in 2003. He had spent more than two years working on the Tony Grove Project, helping map caves cut by water seeping through the soft limestone. Shurtz noticed the swirled snow Bowden and Haskett had described, and he wondered about the breeze that had twisted the crystals. Shurtz climbed a wall in the pit and found an air passageway. Not much of an opening at first, just a narrow tunnel in the wall.

And the tunnel led … down.

Deception Pit had deceived everyone once again. Instead of being only 260 feet deep, it opened into a series of passageways and chambers. Beyond the snow cone lay the Ice Box, Leaky Faucet Pit, Black Rain Canyon, Zigzag Canyon, Frayed Knot Falls, and so on to the very bottom, where a small pool collected in the appropriately named It Can't End Here Room.

Shurtz told an Ogden newspaper the network of passageways is cold (a constant 38°F) and wet. He and his father, Dave, christened one chamber the High and Dry Room because it is the last place where Ryan said he felt "warm and happy." Beyond, rushing water nearly fills a bottleneck, leaving only a foot of air. "You're basically sticking your lips to the ceiling," Shurtz said. "If it [the water level] raises about a foot, then you're done." The route drops gently after the squeeze and stays soggy until it ends, apparently, at the pool.

There, at the clear blue terminal sump, Shurtz and other explorers measured the depth at 1,227 feet, making the cave the ninth deepest in the United States. The explorers christened their discovery "Main Drain," an expression of hope that it would be the

THE CALM SURFACE OF TONY GROVE LAKE REFLECTS THE SHORELINE CLIFFS AT SUNRISE.

PRECEDING PAGES:
LUPINES AND INDIAN
PAINTBRUSH FLANK A
MOUNTAIN BIKER'S TRAIL
IN LOGAN CANYON.

grail, the central drainage of all the caves near Tony Grove. Ninety caves, several of them hundreds of feet deep, had been cataloged as of 2006. The name "Deception Pit" now refers only to Main Drain's entrance pit.

Tony Grove's limestone layer is 1,600 feet deep beneath the entrance to Main Drain. If the cave drops straight to the bottom of the limestone, it would be in the same class as New Mexico's Lechuguilla Cave, at 1,604 feet the deepest in the continental United States, said Tony Grove Project Director Jon Jasper, a scientist who works at Timpanogos Cave National Monument near Provo. To go even deeper, explorers would have to find a passageway through rock strata that dip 15 degrees toward Wood Camp Spring. Fluorescent dye dropped in Main Drain's terminal sump appears in the spring, which is 3,000 feet lower than the cave entrance. However, for explorers to follow Main Drain that far, they would have to hope the cave extends seven miles and breaks through an insoluble quartzite layer.

Main Drain is not for the amateur spelunker. It contains nearly vertical passages measuring hundreds of feet, as if cut by a drill bit turned in the hands of a giant. The walls are jagged, the darkness complete, the descents nerve-wracking, and the explorers' necessary stamina Herculean. Survey trips to the bottom and back can take as much as 14 hours.

Aside from the specialized skills and equipment crucial for exploration, spelunkers also need the location of Main Drain. Jasper's in no hurry to provide that, as the location of caves on federal land such as the national forest is exempt under the Federal Cave Resource Protection Act from disclosure under federal freedom-of-information laws.

CARRYING OUT AN
ANCIENT PARTNERSHIP,
A CLARK'S NUTCRACKER
RETRIEVES ONE OF ITS
CACHED PINE NUTS FOR
FOOD, NEAR RIGHT, WHILE
LEAVING OTHERS TO
SPROUT UNDISTURBED. A
GIANT LIMBER PINE IN
LOGAN CANYON,
OPPOSITE, DEPENDS
ON THE BIRD TO SPREAD
ITS SEEDS.

TWIN CREEK TO FRANKLIN BASIN

DARK LINES ON THE
PETALS OF STICKY
GERANIUM, A COMMON
FLOWER AMID HIGH-
COUNTRY SAGEBRUSH,
DIRECT BEES TOWARD
THE NECTAR AT THE
FLOWER'S CENTER.

For the foreseeable future, the best and safest way to enjoy Main Drain and other caves like it is vicariously through the stories and photos of those able to reach the bottom and return. "These caves are definitely not touristy caves," Jasper said, "but they're for the true explorers."

MILE MARKER 481

Tony Grove took its name not from any Anthony, but rather from the swanky, wealthy, "tony" Logan residents who summered there in the 1890s. In particular, the Thatcher family, a prominent clan of bankers, spent several weeks each summer camping in the cool shade near the high-altitude lake.

Every July and August, the fields of wildflowers north of the lake make their case for being "tony" in their own right. Jim Clow, an accomplished amateur photographer who lives in Logan, said the flowers outshine anything he's ever seen at Yellowstone, and he's visited the national park more than 40 times. The first time he saw Tony Grove's wildflowers in bloom, he spent the better part of three days photographing them.

Botanist Laurel Anderton, a slender woman with round-framed eyeglasses, set out on a July morning to hike from Tony Grove to White Pine Lake, nearly due north, and pick out the different species in bloom. She carried a plastic kitchen container with a snap-on lid. She had placed a damp paper towel inside. Interesting specimens get added to the bowl whenever she hikes; at home she dries and presses the plants between sheets of newsprint and cardboard for examination, classification, and storage. In her upstairs cabinets she has about 1,300 pressings, which she collected everywhere between Chihuahua, Mexico, and Canada's Northwest Territories. She only collects plants when she's certain that taking one won't adversely affect the population; rare and semirare species she leaves untouched.

For one of the first times all summer, cars and trucks filled the parking lot at the trailhead as she set out on the hike. An Audubon Society group had decided to check out the flowering plants encircling the lake at Tony Grove. In addition, a dribble of horses and hikers, along with the occasional mountain biker, moved along the trail through meadows, glacial bowls, and tree-covered slopes en route to White Pine Lake. Anderton shrugged, she prefers the solitude of hiking in what she calls "naked dog country," meaning places so remote she can take the collars off her dogs and let them run free. She had left her two mutts, Zach and Zeke, at home, but that didn't change the sentiment.

The first quarter-mile above the parking lot led through clumps of western wallflower, serviceberry, and snowberry, as well as the ubiquitous sticky geranium and sage. The wallflower, a member of the mustard family, features bright clumps of yellow blooms that are surprisingly fragrant. "Worth a whiff," Anderton said. Finding a sweet cicely herb with its clusters of tiny white flowers, she picked a leaf and crushed it. The scent of licorice perfumed the air.

The number of observable wildflower varieties quickly reached several dozen as the rocky trail rose toward an open view of Mount Gog and Mount Magog, or "Dog and My Dog," as Anderton playfully called them. Every color had its representative. Besides the western wallflower, yellow leaped from the petals of cinquefoil, mule's ear, balsamroot, and glacier lily, a drooping little flower whose peppery leaves make a good lettuce substitute for sandwiches. For orange, there was the semiparasitic Indian paintbrush. For red and magenta, there were scarlet gilia and elephanthead, the latter a figwort whose petals resemble pachyderm ears framing a trunklike projection. Its Latin genus, *Pedicularis*, comes from the scientific name for lice because folklore once held that animals eating it would get infested. Anderton speculated that because animals don't eat elephanthead unless other plants are unavailable, the flower would likely be ingested by beasts already thin, sickly, and louse-ridden. Hence, the connection that mistook cause and effect.

For blue, the trail had Wasatch beardtongue, bluebell, and forget-me-not. For purple, there were the sugary, drooping bells of hairy clematis and sharp spikes of the larkspur. For white, the bistort, columbine, Jacob's ladder, and the appropriately named death camas, which resembles the edible blue camas. For black, the western coneflower. And for green, the green gentian and towering fingers of false hellebore, the latter plant so poisonous that it has been known to sicken people who drink water that has passed through its fields, Anderton said.

Other plants offered good nutrition for those who knew what to look for. Anderton said she and her husband once gathered and boiled piles of bulbs from a field of spring beauties, a tiny white flower that covers the forest floor. They taste starchy, like a potato. Berries of the Utah honeysuckle and varieties of currant also are edible.

As the trail descended, Anderton stopped beside a patriarch of evergreens, its girth as wide as a door. "Do you know how to tell a spruce from a fir?" she asked. She plucked needles from the tree, as well as from a different species a few yards away, and held them out. "If you grab a spruce branch, you'll say 'Ouch,'" she said. "Just remember, 'Flat, friendly fir' and 'Square, sharp spruce.'" Fir needles are flat, like swords, but their tips bend softly on the fingertip. Spruce needles are square in cross-section, and they jab the flesh like, well, needles. The trail descending to White Pine Lake has magnificent specimens of both.

Anderton also pointed out limber pines, named for the flexibility of their limbs. Several of them sometimes grow in one spot, their fused trunks suggestive of a freakish lab accident in a sci-fi movie. The culprit is not a mad scientist, but rather an industrious bird known as Clark's nutcracker.

"I saw to day [a] Bird of the woodpecker kind which fed on Pine burs it's Bill and tale white the wings black every other part," wrote explorer William Clark after becoming the first Euro-American to spot *Nucifraga columbiana* ("nut-breaker of the Columbia") in 1805. Clark was a good hand with a gun and boat, but his partner in the Corps of Discovery, Meriwether Lewis, had the better ornithology credentials. Lewis fixed Clark's error and correctly placed the bird in the family that includes crows and jays. Large for a songbird, the nutcracker grows to be about 11 inches from its sturdy black beak to its ebony tail. It lives in the high woods of the West and announces its presence with a short series of *kraaks*.

While it's not the most melodious or beautiful of birds, Clark's nutcracker plays a crucial role in the life of Rocky Mountain forests. The species has evolved a powerful beak to pry seeds from the ripe cones of limber pines, which grow in abundance in Logan Canyon, as well as whitebark pines more common to the north. The bird can transport several seeds at a time in a pouch under its tongue. A single Clark's nutcracker buries up to 30,000 seeds in a year, scattering them in hundreds of hidey-holes. In winter and spring, the nutcracker returns to about two-thirds to three-quarters of its caches to gather food for itself and its young. Some scientists theorize the bird deliberately leaves some caches untouched as a precaution against bad winters.

Undisturbed pine nuts send forth new trees, singly and in tight clumps. That's a good thing for limber and whitebark pines; the trees' wingless seeds would fall straight down and rot instead of spreading to new locations if it weren't for Clark's bird. Nutcrackers require pine nuts to survive the winter; limber pines need the birds to help them reproduce. In assisting each other, bird and tree perform a waltz of survival every year in Logan Canyon.

At the end of the 3.3-mile trail, White Pine Lake nestles in a limestone basin beneath Gog and Magog, both 9,700-foot peaks. On a calm day, the shallow, green lake is like a polished mirror, reflecting the bright, white band of quartzite that connects the

HORSE AND RIDER DESCEND TOWARD WHITE PINE LAKE ALONG A PATH COVERED WITH WILDFLOWERS.

BURIED TREASURE?

North of the remote White Pine Lake lies the even more remote Steam Mill Lake. The lake and its canyon take their name from a steam boiler abandoned long ago by a logging company. According to legend, the canyon hides a fortune in gold coins stolen during a Wells Fargo robbery more than a century ago. Historian Newell J. Crookston's brief account of the robbery, "The Rainbow's End," tells of an old-timer known only as "Pete" who related the story in 1922. Pete and three other men had robbed the stage near Montpelier, Idaho, and fled with $60,000 in gold. One man kept his $20,000 share, while Pete and the third accomplice buried their portion in Steam Mill Hollow. Pete and the third man were caught and sent to prison, where the third man died. According to Crookston, Pete returned after more than two decades to try to retrieve his treasure but could never locate it. "As far as is known, it still lies hidden in the earth where Pete buried it," Crookston wrote.

More is known about another robbery at Montpelier, just north of Bear Lake, because it was the first carried out by the Wild Bunch. Outlaw Butch Cassidy and his gang held up the Bank of Montpelier in August 1896 and calmly rode away afterward. The robbery netted perhaps $16,500 in gold, silver, and currency, although Montpelier residents argue over the details. A deputy sheriff gave chase on a borrowed bicycle before giving up. Cassidy got away; accomplice Bob Meeks, a local resident who was recognized during the holdup, served time until 1912.

BUTCH CASSIDY, ABOVE, POSES WITH THE WILD BUNCH, BELOW (AT FRONT RIGHT).

two mountains. The water is cold, even in midsummer. Small wonder, as Anderton heard a rumble from the slopes of Magog and looked up to spy a snowball the size of a small car break off a patch of white and roll into the trees beside the lake.

It's a steep hike to climb from the lake back to the altitude of Tony Grove. As the sun rose high, Anderton removed the detachable legs from her pants, turning them into shorts. She paused along the trail and plucked a fleshy green stem with a complicated crown. Anderton folded the stem twice so it would fit in her collection container, and popped on the lid. After she pressed it and dried it, she said, she would try to figure out what it was. Examining and cataloging dried plants are a favorite pastime during Logan's winter months. When wildflowers are nowhere to be found, she can remind herself of the glories of summer.

MILE MARKER 482

Ask fly-fishing fans about the movie *A River Runs Through It*, and you'll find some who loved it and some who hated it.

Chances are, the latter ones took up the sport long before the 1992 film about the fly-fishing sons of a Montana minister. After swooning over the movie's lush riverbank scenery and drinking in its visual poetry about the perfect cast, thousands of wannabes rushed into the icy streams of the West. The secret was out, and in some special places, the solitude was gone.

"It became a granola thing," said Bryan Whitaker, co-owner of RoundRocks Fly Fishing in Logan and a Utah fisherman for nearly five decades. "Every yuppie who was anybody went out and bought a pair of Simms waders and a Sage rod and all the expensive equipment, and they found a guide and went fly-fishing."

The fad has cooled a bit, but the Upper Rockies remain a premier destination for true disciples. Southeastern Idaho, Wyoming, and the canyons of Utah rank just below Montana in the levels of fly-fishing heaven. Whitaker said Logan Canyon is the most popular site for his store's customers because of its abundance of trout, 30 fishable miles, extreme beauty, and easy access to its riverbanks from the highway. Other rivers have wonderful scenery and great fishing, but they can be reached only by a long boat journey. In Logan Canyon, fly-fishing aficionados pull off the highway and pull up their waders.

"If a magazine were to devote an issue to Utah fly-fishing, the Logan River could easily be chosen as the centerfold," crowed *The Flyfisher's Guide to Utah*, one of a series of reference books on American angling. "Logan Canyon in the height of its golden-aspen, crimson-oak autumn glory, invites photographers, inspires

LAST UNSPOILED PLACE

poets, and compels visitors to contemplate lofty issues. The fishing typically ranges from decent to excellent."

Most fish aren't big because much of the river is narrow and fast. Cutthroat trout rank as the most prized native fish. Rainbow, brook, and brown trout, also popular, were introduced to the Logan River, and rainbows still are stocked regularly in the lakes behind First, Second, and Third Dams. RoundRocks displays a photograph of an eleven-pound brown trout on its wall, taken at Second Dam, to provide inspiration. Whitaker said a customer who took him up on recommendations for flies quickly caught a seven-pound brown and dubbed it "troutzilla." One- and two-pound trout are the norm.

The Logan River is cold and rich in minerals, stimulating a healthy population of mayflies, caddis flies, stone flies, and midges for fish to eat. The surroundings change from the canyon mouth to the meadows of Franklin Basin, but it's all beautiful, from the narrow rock walls of the lower canyon to the deep gorge at mile marker 474 to the U-shaped, glacier-sculpted valleys near Tony Grove, Whitaker said.

"Every spot has its own character," he observed. "It's almost like every part of the river has its personality."

One of the most popular sites lies above Red Bank, above the turnoff for Tony Grove. At this location the Logan River, flowing south out of Idaho, joins with Beaver Creek at Franklin Basin and makes a hard right turn to parallel the highway toward Logan. The wall of orange-ochre conglomerate above the river gives the site its name. The run from Franklin Basin to Red Banks resembles a miniature Madison River (a tributary of the Missouri River that is known worldwide for its trout) where cutthroat play amid boulders and riffles. The water is closed to fishing from the first of January through the second Saturday in July to protect the spawning grounds of the native cutthroat. By the time the river opens, the summer heat has loosed an explosion of tiny bugs. As the trout rise to take a fly, the beauty of fishing in a mountain stream expands to include the pleasure of watching a fish break the surface and dance.

Conventional wisdom suggests tying flies that resemble the hordes swirling around the stream. If the fish are gorging themselves on caddis flies, for example, a well-tied caddis lure seems likely to succeed in getting a strike. However, Whitaker finds success in making lures that stand out. Lures that look like oversize insects can attract a fish if it's been doing nothing but nibbling hors d'oeuvres.

BRYAN WHITAKER PREPARES TO CAST A FLY INTO THE LOGAN RIVER, WHICH ABOUNDS IN BROOK, BROWN, CUTTHROAT, AND RAINBOW TROUT.

"They've been eating these little tiny bugs," Whitaker said, trying to see through the eyes of a Logan River trout. "They're sitting there in the water, and the water is bringing bugs over the top of them, all day long. I call it 'eating peas off a conveyor belt.' They've been doing that all day, and in the middle of the summer, some poor young grasshopper lands on top of the water, and floats over them … and it's like a Hershey bar. And they go for it. They're looking for a big hunk of protein."

Whitaker was 12 years old when his father took him fishing for the first time, in the Uinta Mountains below Wyoming's southwestern corner. He treasures those memories. While talking about fly-fishing on a February afternoon at RoundRocks, seated beside a picture window overlooking the Logan River, Whitaker showed off his father's old fly rod. He planned to fix its broken tip and put it on the wall of the shop.

Another fly fisherman, Rob Kempton, is passing on the sport to his children. He said he gets more enjoyment out of watching his two sons catch trout in a mountain stream than he finds in his own fly-fishing. He has reason to be proud: High-school senior Cody, an expert at casting, set the family's record by catching and releasing 81 fish in one day, with one fly, near Lake Tahoe on the California-Nevada border.

Kempton drove a truck for 27 years in Sacramento before moving to Cache Valley. The difference between California and Utah astonished him. Utah is "so much cleaner," unspoiled by trash and debris, he said, and the fishing streams are wide open compared with California's crowds. On a late Saturday afternoon, Rob and Cody Kempton parked their pickup truck near Spawn Creek on the Temple Fork and discovered they were the only ones on the river. "It's a little, dinky thing, but it's full of trout," Rob explained. And appropriately named. In spring, he has seen lots of trout pairing up in Spawn Creek's shallow water.

The Kemptons slowly walked upstream, rods and reels in hand. Trout face upstream to search for food floating down, Rob explained, and they get spooked if they see anyone approach. The Kemptons' plan was to drop dry flies in front of the stream's numerous cutthroat and brown trout, catch as many as they could, and then release them. They hoped to fool the fish into striking at a small hopper made of deer hair, turkey feather, and pheasant tail.

Cody glimpsed a shimmering shadow under a bush at the stream's edge.

"Stay low, buddy. Stay directly behind him if you can," Rob said softly. With a ten o'clock-to-two o'clock pivot of his fore-

arm above the elbow, Cody dropped a fly a few inches above the shadow. The water exploded as a cutthroat snapped at the barbless lure. Cody netted the eight-inch fish, turned the trout sideways to verify the red slash on its throat that gave it its name, and then carefully removed the hook and dropped the fish back in the water.

"Some people spend thousands of dollars for a reel, vest, pole and waders, but they won't spend $50 on a lesson," Rob said of the secret of his son's success. He taught Cody how to cast before the boy set foot in a stream, and it showed. Cody pulled trout after trout out of the swift, cold creek water. His dad watched, approvingly.

Even if father and son had caught nothing, it would have been a good day, strolling toward the high-country beaver ponds at the creek's headwaters amid the lush, green hillsides of Logan Canyon.

CHOOSING THE RIGHT FLY IS PART SCIENCE, PART ART. BRYAN WHITAKER, CO-OWNER OF A LOGAN FLY-FISHING SHOP, DISPLAYS A FEW OF HIS OPTIONS.

THE "RIGHT PLACE"

In Salt Lake City I found to my surprise that Mormons were people," Ernie Pyle wrote in a nationally syndicated newspaper column.

Pyle, a roving reporter of the 1930s who became the nation's most celebrated combat journalist of World War II, said he had "innocently assumed that they were a strange race you couldn't talk with—cold, bluenosed, mystic, and belligerent. They're nothing of the sort; they're just like anybody else." Mormons—more formally, members of the Church of Jesus Christ of Latter-day Saints—boasted some of "the orneriest bastards alive" as well as "the friendliest people on earth," Pyle quoted a Mormon friend as saying.

Pyle wrote about Mormons shortly after driving into Utah, the last state he hadn't previously visited. The fact that Utah occupied the bottom of his list was not particularly surprising; the desert state lies between a towering mountain range on the east and an alkaline desert to the west, and it was one of the last to get good roads. Mormon pioneers who settled Utah appreciated such isolation. It allowed them to practice their religion free from persecutions they had suffered, and fled, in the East.

If he were alive today, Pyle could meet Mormons nearly anywhere. Their church has grown from fewer than a million members in the late 1930s to more than 12 million in the new century. Slightly more than half live

JAY SCHVANEVELDT, PULLING A HANDCART, AND FAMILY RE-ENACT THE TREK OF MORMON PIONEERS TO THE SALT LAKE VALLEY IN 1847 DURING A LOGAN PARADE.

outside the United States, and missionaries comb the planet for converts. Still, Utah and Mormons go together in the public imagination. Julie Hollist, director of Cache Valley's Visitors Bureau, said typically she gets asked two questions when she travels abroad and tells people she's from Utah: Is she Mormon, and does she know singer Donny Osmond, one of the state's most famous natives? (The answers: Yes. No.)

The church traces its origins to Joseph Smith, a farm boy and prophet who received spiritual visions, beginning in 1820 in upstate New York when he was 14 years old. God and Jesus appeared in his first vision. Later, Smith said an angel named Moroni directed him to dig up and translate a golden book telling the history of some of North America's earliest inhabitants. Smith said the Book of Mormon, as the history was called, had been compiled and edited by Mormon, the father of Moroni. Smith and his followers

THE LOGAN TEMPLE, OPPOSITE, LIKE ALL LDS
TEMPLES, IS OPEN ONLY TO THE FAITHFUL.
SALT LAKE CITY'S TEMPLE SQUARE, PICTURED
IN 1912, TOP, ATTRACTS VISITORS FROM
AROUND THE WORLD. A PIONEER DAY PARADE,
CIRCA 1928, MIDDLE, JAMS THE STREETS OF
LOGAN. RIGHT, LOGAN TABERNACLE TAKES
SHAPE IN THE MID-1880S.

officially organized their church in Fayette,
New York, in April 1830. Members believe it
is the only church taking its authority directly
from God, and thus restoring the original
church of Jesus Christ.

LAST UNSPOILED PLACE

LOGAN'S ORIGINAL DOWNTOWN, TOP,
EMERGED FROM THE 19TH CENTURY WITHOUT
LOSING ITS CHARM. TODAY, MAIN STREET, BOT-
TOM, MAINTAINS THE FEEL OF AN UNCOMPLI-
CATED WESTERN TOWN.

Certain practices set Mormons apart. Devout church members follow the Word of Wisdom, a divine revelation proscribing the use of alcohol, tobacco, coffee, and tea. The church doesn't have professional preachers or ecclesiastical vestments; instead, followers are organized in stakes and wards, with each ward's services presided over by laymen who temporarily take the post of bishop. Only men are eligible to hold offices of authority known as the Aaronic and Melchizedek priesthoods.

Beliefs include the reunion of family members in the afterlife and the opportunity for people to be baptized into the church, through proxy, after death. A fraction of Mormon men also took more than one wife until the church stopped sanctioning "plural marriages" in 1890. Cache Valley had its share of polygamist— or, more properly, *polygynist*—families. The great-granddaughter of William H. Maughan contributed a story to the Utah State University folklore collection sketching one of the difficulties of having multiple wives. Maughan, first mayor of the Cache Valley town of Wellsville, had six of them, as well as nearly fifty children who grew to adulthood. Meeting a group of kids at play one day, he tried to name each child's father. He asked one, "And who do you belong to?" The child replied, "To you!"

Some diehards insisted on taking extra wives after 1890, but they were excommunicated. Today, knots of polygamists still live in remote corners of the Intermountain West; however, the church disavows any connection to them.

Friction between the early church and its neighbors forced Smith and his followers out of New York, Ohio, and Missouri. After the Mormons settled in Nauvoo, Illinois, rumors that Smith practiced polygamy (true, it turned out) contributed to a charged atmosphere of religious, political, and economic discord centering on the church's growing influence. A mob killed the prophet in 1844 but could not kill his church. Brigham Young, an early follower of Smith's, led the faithful across the Plains to seek a safe and secure home. He found it on July 24, 1847, when he saw the Valley of the Great Salt Lake and proclaimed, "This is the right place." Young sent out church members to establish colonies, leading to the settlement of Cache Valley.

Mormon settlers dug canals out of solid rock in Logan Canyon to irrigate the valley for their crops and livestock. They hewed stone and timber to build their homes, businesses, church buildings, and schools. And they played as hard as they worked, in activities ranging from acting and singing to athletics. Logan's most famous natives all made their names in public performances. Actor John Gilbert (1899–1936), born to a Mormon mother, became one of Hollywood's first leading men, rivaling Rudolph Valentino in popularity. Merlin Olsen (b. 1940), a Mormon, starred at defensive tackle for Utah State University and the Los Angeles Rams before taking up acting. And tenor Michael Ballam (b. 1951), a Mormon who still lives in Logan, has performed more than 70 major operatic roles throughout the world.

CHAPTER 5

FRANKLIN BASIN TO BEAR LAKE

LAST UNSPOILED PLACE

⬡ **CHAPTER 5** ⬡

FRANKLIN BASIN TO BEAR LAKE

Bryan Lundahl unpacked his avalanche probe in March 2006 for the first time in his nearly 15 years of running Beaver Creek Snowmobiles and Lodge near the summit of Logan Canyon.

Lundahl had killed the engine on his 600-cubic-centimeter Ski Doo in a remote grove of fir trees in Pat Hollow, just north of the Utah-Idaho state line. So did his three companions, who had hired Lundahl to guide them there on a sightseeing trip. Unlike Lundahl, who moved easily in a bright yellow coat with black trim, his three customers picked their way across the snow in black zip-up snowmobiling suits, black boots, black gloves, and dark helmets and goggles—outfits suggesting a cross between ninja warriors and a squad of *Star Wars* Imperial Storm Troopers.

Lundahl knelt in a foot of fresh, soft powder and removed his emergency kit. Aligning the probe's alternating white and purple foot-long metal sections, he quickly fashioned a ten-foot pole and began to pierce the snow.

It was a little after noon, and the aquamarine sky, wire-brushed with cirrus clouds, shimmered through the crystal-frosted boughs overhead. The thin air at 8,600 feet barely stirred, while sunlight picked out a dusting of diamondlike flakes in a snowy clearing 20 yards to the north. If not for the task at hand, the mood might have suggested a Norman Rockwell painting.

Lundahl began near a collection of branches someone had laid atop the snow as a marker. Again and again, for five minutes, he pushed the pole down, searching. He began to sweat with exertion; his face glistened even after he removed his head covering and gloves.

"That's good dirt, there," he said, extracting the probe to reveal a clump of grass and earth the size of a walnut, brought up from nine feet down. A moment later, the probe hit stone. Then, stone again.

With a collapsible shovel from his emergency kit, Lundahl began removing the snow around the pile of branches. He dug a small, round hole, piling the extracted snow around the cavity. After a few minutes, the shovel struck something he had not expected to find.

Out came a tan, cloth cap advertising the tiny town of Sopchoppy, Florida. In ink, someone had written on the bill,

BREAKING A TRAIL NEAR THE TOP OF LOGAN CANYON, BACKCOUNTRY SKIER BRYAN DIXON LEAVES A DISTINCTIVE PRINT IN THE SNOW.

PRECEDING PAGES: SEEN FROM ATOP LOGAN CANYON, BEAR LAKE DISPLAYS ITS DISTINCTIVE BLUE COLOR THROUGH A SCREEN OF CONIFERS.

THE 1953 CRASH OF A
KOREAN WAR MILITARY
TRANSPORT PLANE IN PAT
HOLLOW KILLED 40 AND
SCATTERED DEBRIS,
INCLUDING THIS PIECE OF
WING, OVER A REMOTE
MOUNTAINSIDE.

"Placed in memory of Bruce Malcolm Kemp. 22 years old. Psalm 23. Sept. 28, 2003." A scribbled note on the cap said Kemp had loved his Florida home.

Kemp was heading toward home on a frigid night in January 1953 when his Curtis C-46 military transport plane, en route from Seattle to Cheyenne, Wyoming, crashed into Pat Hollow, killing all 37 soldiers and 3 crew members on board.

Lundahl was probing not for recent victims of winter tragedy, but rather for an encounter with history. His pole had struck the top of a six-and-a-half-foot-tall stone memorial dedicated at the site in 1967 by Gordon B. Hinckley, later to be president of the Church of Jesus Christ of Latter-day Saints. During the summer, when snowy barriers give way to forest trails of pine needles and alpine meadows, visitors to the crash site leave personal mementoes atop the stone. More than a half century after the plane virtually disintegrated on the mountaintop west of St. Charles, Idaho, visitors continue to find pieces of the fuselage and small personal items in the earth. Many are placed reverently atop the memorial.

The plane's flight log indicated it had been packed. Thanks to military precision, all of the passengers had last names beginning with the letters H, J, or K, from James Hardin to John King.

The soldiers and their luggage, heading home from the battlefields of the Korean War, had pushed the plane's weight to about 400 pounds above the limit it had been designed to carry aloft. Just before 1 a.m. January 7, the plane left Boeing Field on the first leg of a journey intended to take it to South Carolina, the jumping-off point for the soldiers' return to their loved ones in the southern states. The pilot radioed a report at 3:58 a.m. to the airfield at Malad City, Idaho, northwest of Logan and about 35 miles from Pat Hollow. All was well as the transport cruised southeast at 13,000 feet. Within the hour, the crew members expected to fly over Rock Springs, Wyoming.

They vanished into silence.

Their disappearance touched off a search by air patrol and civilian volunteers. After five days of combing the Bear River mountains, on January 12, one of the pilots spotted a rubber tire.

The plane had disintegrated on impact. Although there was no fire and no explosion, little remained recognizable except the tail section. Medics parachuted to the site, but there were no survivors. In fact, there were hardly any bodies to speak of amid the pulverized remains of the plane.

"I noticed a Bible at the scene of the crash," wrote L. A. Ripplinger, a staff member of the Logan Herald Journal who was one of the first Cache Valley residents on the scene. "There were also cards. There were many other items, most of which couldn't be identified. Some airplane seats, some trouser pieces with a hip bone jutting from one pant leg. And a lot of small segments of plane and equipment, scattered over the area of an acre." Another reporter wrote of seeing faces sticking out of the snow, and a boot with the leg still inside. One victim's torso still was wrapped in a black coat cut in the Korean style, embroidered with a dragon on the back.

Strangely, the C-46 headed into the mountaintop from the southeast to the northwest. The pilot may have been attempting to return to Malad City for an emergency landing. The Civil Aeronautics Board found no clues indicating engine trouble. Instead, ice forming on the wings apparently had reduced the lift of the already overloaded plane and brought it down.

The crash site was so remote and the conditions so difficult— deep snow, frigid cold, and bodies scattered in pieces—the Army decided to wait until the spring thaw to remove the victims. The 58th Quartermaster Depot Unit, based in Ogden, moved onto the site with the aid of a snow-traction machine, set up a base, and stood guard until the snow melted. They would remove the last human remains in June.

Making the crash doubly tragic were the delayed holiday reunions awaiting the Korean War veterans at their homes. Lundahl, who guides visitors through remote areas of Logan Canyon, shepherded the sister and niece of victim Lawrence Johnson to the site one summer more than four decades after the crash. They had driven from their home in the Carolinas to lay flowers on the monument. "Big tears ran out of her eyes," Lundahl recalled. "They told the story of looking forward to Lawrence coming home for Christmas, and the Army kept delaying it and delaying it. They learned he had died by seeing his name scrolling off the television screen." The family had kept their Christmas tree for nearly two extra weeks so Johnson could enjoy it upon his return.

Johnson's relatives thanked Lundahl with a gift of homemade berry jam. It arrived at Christmas.

Another relative of a victim, the widow of Pearl "J.P." Kelley, visited Pat Hollow with her husband's mother in May 1953 with the assistance of Ada and Lamont "Junior" Pugmire of St. Charles. Lamont, a member of the Bear Lake Rangers riding club, was one of the first to see the disintegrated plane. He had learned about a radio message from the spotters who found the wreckage and recognized their description of the location. The sheriff of Bear Lake County, Idaho, deputized the Rangers to go to the scene of the crash. Pugmire and eleven other Rangers rode horses toward Pat Hollow but were halted by deep snow. While eight stayed behind, Lamont and three others snowshoed the rest of the way, joining the paramedics on site. Lamont snatched a fluttering piece of paper amid the chaos and realized it was a personal letter. "Dear Joe," read the note from Yvonne Kelley to her husband. "I've been down to see your father, and he's not very good." The soldiers on site told him not to take anything, so Lamont left the letter. When a heavy snow began to fall, Pugmire and the other Rangers left the hollow and returned to their eight friends waiting with the horses.

"We told them what it was like," Pugmire said. "They wanted to see it too, but they couldn't make it in. I was tired. When I got home, my wife said, 'What was it like?' but it was just too awful to describe."

Later, the Pugmires saw a news report out of Seattle that said one of the men on the ill-fated plane, Pearl Kelley, had mailed a memento home to his wife in Birmingham, Alabama, before he boarded. That was how the Pugmires knew where Yvonne lived. Ada, the postmistress of St. Charles, contacted the postmaster in Birmingham and got in touch with Kelley's family.

Yvonne had met Pearl, the son of an Alabama coal miner, while roller-skating. "I skated all the time," she recalled. "He did not skate. He would come watch me." They married in July 1951. Three months later, he left for service overseas. In Korea, Pearl Kelley served in the front lines in a field artillery battalion and earned a Purple Heart and Silver Star, but he wrote little to his wife about his combat experiences. She planned a party for his homecoming and made plans to buy a new car.

Yvonne learned of her husband's death through her hometown newspaper in Alabama. She bought a copy at a store but didn't read it right away. "I got home and opened it up, and there was a picture and a write-up on J.P.," she said.

The shock took a long time to dissipate. "That mountain took what it didn't need and I did need," she said.

Over the years, she forged a relationship with the Pugmires. They still exchange letters and phone calls, and the woman now named Yvonne Smith—she remarried, then divorced—has visited the Pugmires twice.

"When I'm on my deathbed, the Pugmires will be some of the last people I think about," she said. "These people are my people."

So too is Hal Briggs, a trumpet player and middle-school music teacher for the Logan School District. Briggs often hikes in Logan

MEMBERS OF AMERICAN LEGION POST 58 IN SMITHFIELD, UTAH, FIRE A SALUTE AT THE CRASH SITE OF THE C-46 TO HONOR THOSE KILLED A HALF CENTURY EARLIER.

Canyon, and has seen everything from a wolverine to a mountain lion while hiking his favorite trails. In the early 1990s, he and a French-horn-playing friend drove a pickup truck north of Beaver Mountain toward the C-46 crash site. When the road gave out, they parked and walked the final half mile to Pat Hollow. Even after four decades, they marveled at the remains of the broken fir trees, sheered by the descending plane's impact. They walked north a bit, higher up the slope, and Briggs turned to survey the scene.

"We were standing there, and I turned to look toward the southwest, and I saw just a little glint," he said. "I thought it was part of the plane. I noticed that if I moved six inches in either direction, I couldn't see it any more."

The glint came from light reflecting off a pearl. It had been weathered and chipped, but clearly it belonged to one of the victims. Briggs speculated: Perhaps a soldier completing a tour of duty in the Orient had picked up a pearl to take home to a wife or girlfriend. He didn't think it would be appropriate to leave it atop the monument, so he took it home and kept it in a little box his grandfather had given him. There it stayed for many months, while Briggs tried to figure out how best to give it to a relative of one of the victims. That problem solved itself when he saw a newspaper article about Yvonne Kelley Smith on the 50th anniversary of the crash. The paper said her husband's name was Pearl.

"This is more than coincidence," Briggs recalled saying to himself.

A reporter put Smith in touch with Briggs, and the music teacher arranged to give her the pearl. Smith accepted the gift on behalf of everyone aboard the plane. She keeps it in her curio cabinet, along with Pearl's medals.

"It kind of brings tears to my eyes every time I talk about it," Briggs said. "It makes me almost wonder if I was being directed" to find a pearl amid a site of so much death.

Someday, he said, he'd like to play Taps on his trumpet at the memorial site.

MILE MARKER 487

Luella Seeholzer also wanted to do her part to help after the plane was found. So when she and her husband, Harold, heard a military crew had been dispatched to the crash site, she started to warm a pot of bean soup and make sandwiches.

"Mom said we better take food to them because the military won't have sense enough to bring food along with them," said her son, Ted Seeholzer.

Today, Ted, his wife, and two of his children and their spouses own and operate the 1,100-acre Beaver Mountain ski resort,

IN MEMORY OF

THE CIVILIAN CREW AND 37 MILITARY
PASSENGERS WHO WERE KILLED WHEN A C 46
AIR TRANSPORT CRASHED HERE WHILE ENROUTE
FROM SEATTLE, WASHINGTON TO FORT JACKSON,
SOUTH CAROLINA ON JANUARY 6, 1953.

PILOT   LAURENCE CRAWFORD
FIRST OFFICER   MAXWELL PERKINS
STEWARDESS   DOROTHY DAVIS

HARDIN, JAMES P.   JENKINS, MARVIN
HARDY, ULYSSES   JENKINS, ROBERT, JR.
HARGRETT, HERBERT S.   JINKS, RUSSEL
HARPER, CHARLES A.   JOHNSON, HENRY A.
HARRELL, RALPH D.   JOHNSON, JAMES, JR.
HARVILEY, MATHEW   JOHNSON, LAWRENCE
HATCHER, WALTER, JR.   JOHNSON, ROBERT L.
HENDERSON, WILLIE B.   JOHNSON, ROBERT W.
HENDRIX, RUTHEL O.   JOHNSON, WILLIE E.
HILL, JIMMIE   JONES, JAMES R.
HOLLINGSWORTH, MC LEAN   JONES, JEFF W.
HOLLOWAY, RAYMOND F.   JOSEY, JAMES E.
HUDSON, ARTHUR   JOYNER, WALTER B.
HUDSON, FRANCIS A.   KELLEY, LEROY, JR.
HUMAN, DAVID   KELLEY, PEARL J., JR.
JACKSON, ERNEST   KEMP, BRUCE M.
JAGGERS, MOSES   KENT, JOSEPH O.
JENKINS, HERBERT M.   KING, JOHN M.
        HERZIG, WILFRIED OTTO WALTER PAUL

PRESENTED & ERECTED BY NEPHI J. BUTT — SEPTEMBER 20, 1957

a few miles south of the crash site. It's the oldest family-run ski operation in the country, having been a Seeholzer business since 1939.

The familial feeling that prompted Ted's parents to care for the soldiers at the crash site still defines the Seeholzers' resort. Ted Seeholzer's son Travis and son-in-law Jeff West leave Logan before 5 a.m. in winter to arrive at Beaver Mountain in time to plow the parking lot and groom and check the slopes. Ted's wife, Marge, arrives at 6:30 to open the ticket booth, turn on the heat, and get ready for the first arrivals. Travis's wife, Kristy, updates the resort's Web site. Together, they and Ted's daughter Annette Seeholzer West join Ted in company meetings of six family members. The business used to involve a bigger family, but Ted and Marge borrowed $900,000 a few years ago, at age 68, to buy out his brothers and sisters.

A MARKER AT THE CRASH SITE LISTS THE VICTIMS. EACH SOLDIER ABOARD THE CURTIS C-46 HAD A LAST NAME THAT START-ED WITH H, J, OR K.

Ted admits to being a bit more softhearted than the corporations that run most ski resorts. He's not above giving a refund for a $33 day's pass, if he thinks it's warranted.

"If you got injured, or if you got tired, after half a day, it's very difficult for me to say, 'You bought your ticket, and you use it,'" he said. "If you don't pull my leg, I don't have a problem with it." If he catches someone committing fraud, however—handing a season pass to a friend and then claiming to have forgotten it in order to get a comped ticket for a day—he's not so forgiving. "When we

SKIERS LINE UP FOR THE ROPE TOW DURING THE EARLY YEARS OF OPERATION AT FAMILY-OWNED BEAVER MOUNTAIN.

catch a cheater, we take their pass. We might give it back, and we might not, depending on their attitude. If they're smart in the mouth, they might not get it back."

Ted's father, Harold Seeholzer, helped pioneer downhill skiing in northern Utah. A photograph of Harold and his first skis, bought in 1918, depict them towering over his head, easily nine feet long. Harold hiked and skied in Logan Canyon. So did students at the university and other ski enthusiasts in the valley. Many learned under the tutelage of George Nelson, an athletic trainer who traveled to Utah State Agricultural College from Oslo, Norway, in the 1920s. Students skied in the campus's first winter carnival in 1922, sliding down Old Main Hill and Smart Flats, and took part in ski-jump contests at Spring Hollow in 1930, after the Utah Highway Department kept the road open that far into the canyon. During the 1930s, racers hiked to the top of Mount Logan, on the south side of the entrance to Logan Canyon, and competed to see who could descend the fastest. It took four hours to walk to the top and eight to twelve minutes to reach the bottom.

Harold Seeholzer and other ski enthusiasts selected Beaver Mountain as Logan Canyon's premier real estate for a ski lift. They installed a cable lift on a single slope in the late 1930s. As they had no money to improve a connecting road, skiers had to park at the highway and hike a mile to the lift.

"I remember walking here on my fifth birthday," Ted Seeholzer recalled from his seat inside the resort's toasty ticket booth, insulated from the 20-degree air by newspapers in the walls and a blanket of snow. "I remember sitting and bawling because I was cold, and Dad built a bonfire to keep us warm."

The highway through Logan Canyon stayed open year-round after the winter of 1939-40. For the next few years, to take advantage of the road's easy access, Harold Seeholzer and partner Don Shoup moved southeast to operate a ski lift at Summit Valley in "the Sinks," a series of bowl-like depressions.

Tickets for the 1,500-foot tow cost 50 cents for men and 25 cents for women and children. Summit Valley proved so popular on holidays that Logan police appointed a patrol officer to supervise highway traffic. Other days often were lean. Harold Seeholzer's financial books included daily collection totals of $12 for lift tickets and $7 for Luella Seeholzer's homemade chili and barbecue. "A $39 day up at the Sinks was a big day," Ted said.

Summit Valley lacked potential for growth, so after World War II the family business moved back to Beaver Mountain. The reopened resort's first uphill conveyance consisted of a rope tow attached to the jacked-up rear end of a crashed milk truck.

Public money from a Utah commission intended to boost state recreation set Beaver Mountain on a path toward professional development. A parking lot and a connecting highway made the mountain accessible. Harold Seeholzer, acting on his own after his partner left the business, obtained a special-use permit from the national forest. Seeholzer erected a building, which later became the ticket office, and a homemade paddle lift in 1947. A rope tow followed in 1950, and two volunteer ski patrollers went on duty to

look out for the safety of the weekends-only patrons.

The Seeholzers formed a family corporation a decade later and kept expanding and improving the resort with new buildings and chair lifts. The "Harry's Dream" lift fulfilled a longstanding ambition of Ted's father: To send a chair all the way to the top of the mountain. Unfortunately Harold died, in 1968, before he could see his dream realized in 1970.

Beaver Mountain relies mainly on word-of-mouth advertising, but it's enough to bring an average of 740 skiers a day in a winter season that can stretch from Thanksgiving to Easter. As many as 2,000 people crowd the slopes on holidays. Recent visitors included skiers from France, Germany, and Denmark, as well as winter sports enthusiasts seeking the resort's family treatment. "Treat our customers as guests—treat our guests as friends," says the first page of the employee handbook.

Wendell Liechty, 70 years old in the spring of 2006, joined the all-volunteer Beaver Mountain Ski Patrol in 1952 and has served every winter except for two years in the Army. He began with wooden skis, which he had to constantly wax. They had no bind-

BEAVER MOUNTAIN LOOMS IN THE DISTANCE AS THE HEADWATERS OF THE LOGAN RIVER TRICKLE BETWEEN YELLOW WILLOWS IN UPPER LOGAN CANYON.

PRECEDING PAGES:
A NORDIC SKIER
MAKES HER OWN TRAIL
THROUGH FRESH POW-
DER IN THE MOUNTAINS
OF LOGAN CANYON.

ings—just a toe strap, sometimes augmented with an inner tube that added a little traction. He graduated to modern synthetic-composition skis, but has never made the leap to snowboarding.

"I tried to snowboard, and I worked harder doing that than I ever wanted to work," said Liechty, a retired plumbing wholesaler. "I believe if I had started when I was younger, I would have had a lot of fun."

Sometimes skiers lose their way in clouds, storms, or darkness. Night rescues on Beaver Mountain can get a little "spooky," Liechty said, when he has to ski into pitch-black darkness. He helped find a pair of girls at 3 a.m. on the back of the mountain, and another pair of skiers at 6 in the morning. "They had started a fire to keep warm, and they took off their plastic ski boots," Liechty said. "They hung them by the fire, and they melted and they couldn't get them back on their feet."

NEVER FREEZING, A
SPRING-FED CREEK
IN LOGAN CANYON
FLOWS THROUGH
BOULDERS AND SNOW-
COVERED BRUSH.

Balancing the difficult times are the transcendent moments that dedicated skiers worship.

"A lot of times, when you get to the spring of the year, and it's real cold at night and warm during the day, it settles down the whole mountain," Liechty said. "If you get two inches of corn snow, you can ski anywhere you want. And in shirtsleeve weather." Still, "nothing beats 15 inches of fresh, fluffy powder, and you can get it any time from December to February."

Utah's license plates proclaim it the "Greatest Snow on Earth." It's a light powder, formed in part by the state's dry air, which drivers can practically blow off their windshields with a sneeze. Like any precious resource, Logan Canyon's snow has drawn competing claims.

Snowmobilers and nonmotorized users are like oil and water," said John Louviere, program administrator for USU's Outdoor Recreation Center. "They don't mix whatsoever."

Snowmobile riders and cross-country skiers clashed for decades over their competing claims to the canyon. The snowmobilers wanted broad access to trails and off-trail acreage; skiers wanted large zones free from the noise and pollution of snowmobiles' two-stroke engines. After years of squabbling, the two sides settled their differences in 2006 by endorsing a U.S. Forest Service plan that designated areas for snowmobiles, for nonmotorized users, and for mixed use. Skiers dropped their opposition to the plan only after the Forest Service put 4,000 disputed acres of Franklin Basin, west of Beaver Mountain, firmly in the nonmotorized column.

To Bryan Lundahl, the antagonists have much in common. Both want to experience the canyon's winter wonders. And both enjoy the solitude far from the cities. Skiers take the slow, quiet route to isolation; snowmobilers go faster and louder, but when they reach their inspiration point, they often kill their engines to drink in the white silence.

"The canyon is big enough, there's something for everybody," Lundahl said.

His Beaver Creek Lodge rents horses in the summer and fall and snowmobiles when the snow is deep enough to cover the sage and boulders. "Everyone thinks I have the best job there is," Lundahl said.

Lundahl, who grew up in Cache Valley, knew he always wanted to work outdoors. For a while he dreamed of shoeing horses for a living. At USU, a business professor's class assignment challenged him to do the research necessary to carry out a change of zoning. Lundahl's father told him to take the challenge one step further: to actually execute the proposed change. Lundahl did, and secured

PRECEDING PAGES: ICE
FORMS ON THE LOGAN
RIVER AT DUSK BELOW
CIRRUS AND CIRROSTRA-
TUS CLOUDS.

the necessary permit from the Forest Service to open his lodge. He
started horseback tours from an empty lot in 1991, added snowmobile rentals in 1992, and finished his lodge in 1993.

SnoWest magazine rates the canyon as one of the top snowmobiling destinations in the West. "Probably nowhere in the state of
Utah (and maybe the snowbelt in general) is there a combination
of incredible vistas, unique snow quality and diversity of rideable
terrain than what exists out of the Tony Grove and Franklin Basin
trailheads up Logan Canyon," the magazine said in 2006. Lundahl
touts the quality of the snow and trails, which total more than 300
groomed miles between Bloomington, Idaho, and the Monte
Cristo Mountains to the south. But the off-trail opportunities are
just as impressive, he said. Many customers come from New York
and the Midwest, where the land is flatter and the trails shorter.
Lundahl boasts that he can guide visitors on different day trips for
four consecutive days, setting off in each of four directions.

On a painfully bright day, after spring break at the university,
Lundahl set out a half-day trip in a lazy figure eight that spanned
45 miles of Logan Canyon peaks and valleys. His snowmobile
passed Amazon Hollow, North Sink, Middle Sink, and crested over
a ridge into Peter Sink. It climbed through Dead Man Gulch to stop
at Horse Lake, where a turnoff affords a view of Gog and Magog,
twin mountains named for figures out of the Book of Revelation,
which guard White Pine Lake six miles to the west. The snowmobile zipped across Swan Flats to the Utah-Idaho border, to Ranger
Dip and Red Pine. From nearby St. Charles Peak—named for a
Mormon, or "Saint," pioneer, Charles Rich—a visitor could see the
Teton and Uinta ranges, each a hundred miles away. Then it turned
north on the Old Logan Road, passed over Beaver Creek, and
stopped at the Korean War plane crash site in Pat Hollow before
turning for home.

MILE MARKER 488

If you didn't know to look, you might pass the Amazon mine
without knowing it's there. It sits in Amazon Hollow, east of Beaver
Creek Lodge, accessed by a tree-lined path.

The mine is quiet now, but for a while it bustled with activity.

The Mormon Church urged its members to work at agriculture
instead of mining. After all, pioneers in the desert couldn't eat precious metals. "Stay home and attend to your farms and do not
think of gold mining," Brigham Young told the citizens of
Providence, south of Logan, in 1867. Likewise, Mormon leader
Orson F. Whitney proclaimed, "Who would wish to see … peace-
ful Deseret, the home of a people who had fled for religious free-

dom and quiet … converted into a rollicking, roaring mining camp? Not the Latter-day Saints!"

Nevertheless, the lure of easy money proved tempting. Miners began prospecting at Beaver Creek, a branch of the Logan River high in Logan Canyon, in 1882, and found galena, the gray ore that yields lead. Prospectors also found traces of silver and copper near Logan Cave. Between 1892 and 1897, miners registered 79 claims in Cache Valley, mostly in Logan Canyon. Mines included the Utah Queen, the Surprise, the Bunker Hill, and a vein of galena named the Republican. Perhaps hedging their bets, the Republican's operators opened a new mine and called it the Democrat.

A former banking and geology student at Utah State Agricultural College, H. C. Hansen, found the largest mine by accident. He was exploring Logan Canyon on June 20, 1892, when he happened across a giant boulder of galena. The ore rested on the surface, making its vein easy to trace. Hansen and three other men staked a claim and called their mine the Amazon because they thought it was going to be as huge as the river. Hansen began digging and putting in support timbers. At a fissure, he dropped a rock into a

SMOKE RISING FROM A SHACK AT THE AMAZON MINE INDICATES LINGERING HOPES WITHIN. THE MINE YIELDED ONE LUCRATIVE HAUL IN 1892. THEN, NOTHING.

WORK CREWS AT THE AMAZON MINE, SUCH AS THIS ONE A CENTURY AGO, KEPT DIGGING IN THE DARKNESS WITHOUT SUCCESS AFTER THE FIRST STRIKE.

black chasm. He reported it fell a long time—"like it went to the center of the earth."

Miners drilled 1,200 feet into the Amazon, excavating a shaft that remains today beneath U.S. 89. Despite high hopes, the Amazon yielded exactly one lucrative shipment of ore in nearly a century of on-and-off exploration. Five tons of rock fetched $5,000 in 1892, the high-water mark of mineral exploration in the canyon. That fall, with the election of President William Henry Harrison, who opposed the free coinage of silver, interest in the pursuit of elusive silver waned. Work resumed in 1906 and again in 1920 without result.

Throughout the decades, the Amazon has remained an open hole atop Logan Canyon. It waits, beside the remains of an ancient cabin, for the next dreamer to come along.

MILE MARKER 491

Everyone has a favorite spot in the canyon. John Louviere considers the Jardine Juniper Trail the best suited for all sports, including snowshoeing, hiking, mountain biking, and telemark skiing. He also enjoys Right Hand Fork and Blind Hollow, but is cautious when questioned too closely. "I haven't told you all of the best spots," he told a visitor to his USU campus office. "Some I keep for myself."

College students on a tight budget—and that means most of them—like the Sinks.

The collapse of limestone caverns in the mountains has left oblong depressions in the alpine fields. In winter, these so-called sinks fill with snow, becoming nature's version of urban skate parks. Just past Amazon Hollow, where the highway bends to the south, a series of sinks beckons to winter revelers: North Sink, South Sink, Middle Sink, and—*shudder*—Peter Sink.

North Sink, which parallels the highway, was the site of Summit Valley ski resort during World War II. Today, it still draws skiers and snowboarders. The main difference is, these visitors pay for the ascent not with money for lift tickets, but with the sting of sore muscles.

"Hey, Nolan!" Robert McDaniel, a photography student from South Carolina, yelled to goad his friend, a business major from Tremonton, Utah. "Your Indian name is Big Talk."

For perhaps 20 seconds, Nolan Jensen had been balancing on his snowboard, surveying the miles of snow he could see to the left and right as well as on the floor of North Sink a hundred feet below him. It was 11:30 a.m. on Presidents Day, a day off from books and classes. Ten yards below, a five-foot-high ramp of snow rose from the slope. Jensen and a half-dozen friends had formed the mound with snow shovels and sprayed the front edge with an aerosol can of black paint.

"Don't get hurt," another buddy, liberal arts and sciences major Casey Zundel, teased. "But if you do, we'll take you to the hospital around 2 or 3."

Jensen pushed off, jumped at the black line, and soared into space. He landed perfectly ten yards down the hill, pivoted, and turned to look back at his friends.

"Whoa, that was *rad!* You went high," came a shout from the knot of spectators. Jensen stepped off his board and began the five-minute trek through 18 inches of fresh powder to get in position for another run.

It was a gorgeous day for the students' low-budget version of ski jumping: slightly overcast and 14 degrees Fahrenheit in Logan, a sunnier 7 degrees at the lip of the sink, a few degrees colder in the basin. Friends had assembled at 9:35 that morning at McDaniel's Logan apartment, decorated with posters of Jim Morrison and Quentin Tarantino's *Pulp Fiction*. McDaniel prepared for his trip by fishing two Diet Mountain Dews and a Diet Pepsi out of the fridge—no morning coffee; he's a Mormon—and filling his pock-

PRECEDING PAGES:
NORDIC SKIERS RACE
ACROSS MIDDLE SINK,
ONE OF SEVERAL DEPRES-
SIONS THAT FORM FRIGID
MICROCLIMATES AT THE
TOP OF LOGAN CANYON.

ets with six boxes of Polaroid film. He layered his body with two T-shirts, thermal underwear, jeans, snow pants, an Army coat, gloves, an outer synthetic shell, Army surplus socks, and boots.

For a young man who rarely saw snow in his native Charleston, McDaniel quickly learned the ways of the snowy West. Snow-boarding took longer. His trip to North Sink marked his third time on a snowboard and his first attempting a jump.

When McDaniel took his turn at the line above the ramp, he too paused, just as he had seen Jensen do, and took a deep breath. Then he pushed off.

Whump. Even before his board got to the homemade ramp, McDaniel went down. He stood and started again; this time he hit the black line and wobbled into the air like a wounded pheasant.

Whump. Again.

He got up, smiled, and dusted off the snow. "It's still better than a resort," he said.

MILE MARKER 492

Southwest of North Sink, beyond the trees and up a ridge, lies Peter Sink. Lundahl said a Bear Lake old-timer told him the sink took its name from a miner who tried to homestead. When he did-n't show up after a nasty winter, a search party from Bear Lake went looking for him. The party found him frozen to death.

Peter Sink, at 8,500 feet, is famous for its bone-chilling cold. The bottom, treeless because of the intense cold, is only about 200 feet below the lip. Yet sliding into the basin of Peter Sink is like plung-ing into the Arctic Ocean. Needles of cold stab at exposed flesh. Goggles start to frost over. An icy chill knuckles its way from ankles to thighs.

"Sometimes it's so cold a kind of mist hovers over it," Lundahl said. "When it's like that, I don't go there."

In February 1985, a thermometer in Peter Sink registered 69.3 degrees below zero Fahrenheit. That was seven-tenths of a degree warmer than the lowest reading ever in the lower 48 states, made at Roger's Pass, Montana, in 1954. In such temperatures, exposed flesh freezes within a few seconds. Meteorology researcher Zane Stephens, department head for industrial maintenance and safety management at Bridgerland Applied Technology College in Logan, said he twice has felt the chill of 60 degrees below zero at the sinks. "You can spit ice cubes," he told a newspaper reporter who accompanied him on a midwinter trek to Peter Sink.

Robert Gillies, director of the Utah Climate Center, explained that cold lingers in the bottom of the sinks because of a mix of topography and meteorology. The air at the top of the canyon is cold to begin with, thanks to high altitudes, radiative cooling, and the snow reflecting the sun's energy instead of absorbing it. Adding to those factors is the sink's bowl shape. Cold air, which is heavier than warm air, collects in the bottom.

"Cold air is stable; it doesn't have buoyancy," said Gillies, a native of the Scottish Highlands. "Cold air is happy being cold. It will go down, and stay there."

Frigid air in the sinks—sometimes so cold that a camera's flash illuminates tiny snow crystals forming in the atmosphere—is especially stable when held down by an inversion, a layer of warm air above a layer of cold. Below the inversion a dynamic, unstable layer of air creates some circulation within the sink, but air chilled during the circulation joins the icy pool at the bottom. During winter, the low angle of the sun doesn't provide enough energy to jolt the system into a new pattern.

Gillies considered it inappropriate to accept low-temperature readings from Peter Sink as official weather records. After all, they came from a remote microclimate where nobody lives—at least, not since Peter the miner.

Still, Gillies knows firsthand how cold it gets at Peter Sink. He has visited twice. Once was in the summer, and once in winter,

ALL-DAY TICKETS FOR THE TOW ROPE TO THE TOP COST AS LITTLE AS A QUARTER AT SUMMIT VALLEY, A SKI ATTRACTION IN THE SINKS IN THE 1940S.

BEACHGOERS ENJOY THE
SHORE AND GENTLE
WAVES AT THE WESTERN
EDGE OF BEAR LAKE, EAST
OF LOGAN CANYON.

"which I regret," he said. Of the latter trip, he said in his Scottish brogue, "It was stinking cold."

Above Peter Sink, on one of the highest ridges of Logan Canyon, a snowmobiler can turn off the engine and enjoy the top of the world. Far below shines the surface of Bear Lake, a gleaming shade of turquoise because of calcium carbonate molecules from the ubiquitous limestone suspended in the water. To the north lies Idaho; to the east, Wyoming; to the south and west the ridges and valleys of a magnificent Utah canyon.

The corrugated landscape looks as if a giant had squeezed the surface like an accordion. Surely if Logan Canyon were ironed flat, it

LAST UNSPOILED PLACE

would cover three to four times as much area. Then even its remotest corners could be easily reached by car, bike, or foot. Its simple, hidden joys, long known only to those who take the trouble to explore, might be as beloved as, say, Yellowstone Lake or the trail ridge at Rocky Mountain National Park, which lie beside good roads.

Something wonderful lies in this rough canyon's seeming desire to shield its treasures from casual observers. Logan Canyon yields its secrets only to those who deliberately seek communion with nature in one of the world's last unspoiled places.

The canyon welcomes them—as it welcomed the Shoshone, the mountain men, the Mormons, and all who have come after. With time, it has grown even more beautiful and welcoming. "Old scars left by forest fires are no longer visible, and are covered with a new

BEAR LAKE'S FAMOUS FRUIT

Motorists on U.S. 89 might be tempted to scoff and keep driving when they learn that Garden City, on the edge of Bear Lake, bills itself as the "Raspberry Shake Capital of the West." Just another touristy gimmick, they might think.

Too bad.

Raspberry growers on the western side of the lake, at the exit of Logan Canyon, have produced uniquely large and sweet berries ever since German immigrant Theodore Hildt planted a few canes in the dust nearly a century ago.

The locals shrug when pressed about how the berries, which must picked every day when they ripen in July and August, grow tasty enough to attract up to 20,000 visitors to Garden City's Raspberry Days Festival. Explanations range from cold summer nights to tender loving care to—*ahem*—marketing. It didn't hurt when the *New York Times* and *Washington Post* published sweet nothings about Garden City's raspberry milk shakes. The former called the Bear Lake raspberry the source of the town's "unlikely gastronomic success;" the latter settled for simpler words such as *unique* and *wonderful.*

Bushy dwarf virus, transferred by bees, devastated the crop early in the new century. Growers ripped out the old plants, put in new ones from out of state, and started over. The berries bounced back in three years. Fresh raspberries once again found their way into fast-food cups to be blended with soft ice cream into a mixture so thick it cannot be sucked through a straw. The *Post* described motoring along a Logan Canyon road, with a shake in one hand and a spoon in the other, as a supreme test of driving skills.

Better—and safer—for drivers to pull over, kill the engine, and sit a spell in Garden City. The raspberry milk shake deserves undivided attention.

FOOD CRITICS SWOON OVER THE SWEET, JUICY BERRIES PICKED NEAR BEAR LAKE.

FOXTAIL BARLEY, A GRASS
NATIVE TO UTAH, GROWS
ALONG THE HIGHWAY
HIGH IN LOGAN CANYON.

growth of trees and shrubs," wrote Logan Canyon historian Newell J. Crookston. "Hills that were once denuded of vegetation are almost smothered with foliage. ... [The] forest is recognized as one of the most productive areas in the West for deer, elk, and fish, and is certainly one of the most beautiful recreational canyons to be found anywhere."

Americans marvel at their factories, skyscrapers, and superhighways, which seemingly rival the world's natural wonders. Yet when their spirits run dry, they turn not to monuments of concrete and steel, but rather to the wild places. Places of green leaf and gray stone. Of crashing waters, leaping fish, and animal tracks in red spring mud. Of solitude and silence. In short, places that nourish the soul.

Logan Canyon is such a place.

The *Conservation News* wrote of the canyon, in 1960, a description that still rings true. Along the highway and the river are majestic views of stone and fir. Side canyons stretching from the river "fairly shout an invitation to the hikers, beauty seekers, or geologist who would find in the area a heaven on earth," the *News* said.

"In fact, if the Great Hand had wanted to paint a canyon, it would hardly have traced a more beautiful one than Logan."

THE HEAT IS ON?

Utah is America's second driest state, behind Nevada. So a study suggesting Utah will receive significantly more precipitation in the next century ought to seem like good news.

But there's a catch: The deluge, linked to global warming, would put stress on Utah's human environment. Together, higher regional temperatures and rainfall would reshape the face of Logan Canyon, Cache Valley, and the Valley of the Great Salt Lake, as well as the rest of the Great Basin and northern Rockies.

Ecologist Frederic H. Wagner of Utah State University coordinated the assessment of climate change in the nine-state Rocky Mountain-Great Basin region for the Global Change Research Program, created in response to a 1991 congressional order. Wagner realized he needed a broad range of expertise to study how the region might respond to shifts in long-term weather patterns. "Climate change involves everything in our lives," he said. "Agriculture, climatology, outdoor recreation. ... It's part of everything." He drafted experts in water resources, cultivated agriculture, recreation, and other areas to help gather and analyze data.

Computers at the National Center for Atmospheric Research in Boulder, Colorado, one of the largest climate research labs in America, ran sophisticated modeling programs based on existing climate data in order

CRACKED AND DRY EARTH, EXPOSED BY THE RECEDING GREAT SALT LAKE, STRETCHES TO THE HORIZON AT THE BEAR RIVER MIGRATORY BIRD REFUGE WEST OF CACHE VALLEY.

to forecast the region's future. They projected increases of a minimum of 2.5 to 4.5 degrees Celsius (4.5° to 8.1°F) in the region's seasonal temperatures by the end of the 21st century. Those predictions are based on a widely held assumption that the presence of carbon dioxide, belched from the world's engines of economic growth, will double during the next century. Those same models forecast a minimum increase of 54 percent and a maximum

of 184 percent in mean annual precipitation in the Rocky Mountains and Great Basin.

Wagner acknowledged the uncertainties of predicting the future. However, the projections are bolstered when compared with observed readings that demonstrate a correlation of temperature, precipitation, and carbon dioxide buildup in the 20th century. Research at the U.S. Geological Survey office in Salt Lake City indicated Utah's temperatures rose an average of 3 degrees Fahrenheit during the 20th century, while the state's annual mean precipitation rose 12 percent. Increases were more pronounced north of Utah. Projections point toward a loss of Glacier National Park's namesake ice fields within a few decades and a possible loss of snowpack in the northern Rockies a few decades after that. Snowpacks already are shrinking.

LOGAN CANYON STREAMS, INCLUDING ONE ALONG THE JARDINE JUNIPER TRAIL, LEFT, WILL FLOW EARLIER AND HEAVIER IN SPRING UNDER CLIMATE CHANGES FORECAST BY COMPUTER MODELS. GREENHOUSE GASES, BELCHED FROM NORTHERN CALIFORNIA SMOKESTACKS, RIGHT, AND OBSCURING SALT LAKE CITY, ABOVE, THREATEN PROFOUND CHANGES TO LOGAN CANYON.

"A hundred years from now, there may be no snowpack in Logan Canyon," Wagner said.

The canyon's mix of plant and animal species would change too, he said. A rise in stream temperature would push popular cold-water species such as trout to the relatively chilly mountaintops or possibly replace them altogether with warm-water species such as bass and catfish. However, browsing animals such as native deer and elk would benefit from access to year-round green leaves at high elevations. Forest zones would

THE 1,500-FOOT-LONG SPIRAL JETTY, AN EARTH-WORK COMPLETED IN 1970 BY ROBERT SMITHSON, ACTS AS A GREAT SALT LAKE DEPTH GAUGE. IT ALSO COULD BECOME A BAROMETER OF CLIMATE CHANGE.

expand in the new rainfall, moving upslope to eventually eliminate alpine tundra and downslope to push desert plants onto the valley floors.

The forecast for the next few decades calls for a big increase in precipitation in the Bear River Mountains that frame Logan Canyon. Any snow that does persist is expected to melt earlier in the spring and start falling later in the autumn. Taken together, the changes would have a huge impact on the size and pattern of flow in the Logan River and other streams that feed the Great Salt Lake.

And there, in the remnant of the ice-age Lake Bonneville, the definition of "basin" would become a matter of grave concern. Water flows into the Great Salt Lake, but it doesn't flow out.

"If we get a big increase in precipitation, the Great Salt Lake is going to rise and rise, and the Wasatch Front is going to be in a heap of trouble," Wagner said.

The Great Salt Lake's surface level rose and fell in the latter half of the 20th century, ranging from a low in 1967, when observers thought the lake might disappear, to the years in the late 1980s that locals still call "The Big Wet." That's when precipitation was 12 percent above average. The lake literally lapped at the western edge of Salt Lake City and threatened to submerge the runways of the city's international airport. The city and its suburbs faced isolation from the world in three directions.

Artist Robert Smithson's monumental Spiral Jetty, a 1,500-foot coil of salt-encrusted black basalt rocks at the Great Salt Lake's northern edge, has acted as a sort of depth gauge for Utah precipitation. It was easily visible when Smithson completed it in 1970, at the end of the long dry spell. During the late 1980s, the jetty disappeared. A decade later, thanks to drought at century's end, the lake level fell, its threats to Salt Lake City abated, and Spiral Jetty slowly re-emerged. Art lovers flocked to

the remote site, south of the Golden Spike National Historic Site, to drink in the genius of the counterclockwise swirl of rock Smithson built up in the briny, purple-pink waters.

Raising the lake level a foot or two would once again hide the jetty. Raising it a bit more would bring back memories of the Big Wet. And, Wagner says, a 50 to 100 percent increase in Utah's annual precipitation would turn Salt Lake City's nightmares of the 1980s into reality. Meanwhile, as rising water levels likely shrink the land available for human use along the narrow strip between the Great Salt Lake and the Wasatch Mountains, Utah's population is expected to double, to 4.7 million, by 2050.

The water so desperately prayed for by Utah's Mormon pioneers as they sought to make the desert bloom might then become too much of a good thing.

INDEX

Author's note: I would like to thank Mike Bullock and Julie Hollist for their assistance.

ILLUSTRATIONS CREDITS

1, Phil Schermeister. 2-3, Scott T. Smith. 6-7, Scott T. Smith. 8, Phil Schermeister. 10, Phil Schermeister. 13, Phil Schermeister. 15, Special Collections and Archives, Merrill Library, Utah State University. 16-17, Scott T. Smith. 19, Phil Schermeister. 20-21, Scott T. Smith. 22, NASA/Jesse Allen. 24-25, Phil Schermeister. 27, Scott T. Smith. 28, Library of Congress. 30-31, Scott T. Smith. 33, Phil Schermeister. 34-35, Phil Schermeister. 36, Michael Sweeney. 38-39, Denver Public Library, Western History Collection, X-32282. 40, Library of Congress. 41 (UP), Denver Public Library, Western History Collection, 32297. 41 (LO), Denver Public Library, Western History Collection, 32254. 42, Scott T. Smith. 43, Scott T. Smith. 44-45, Scott T. Smith. 46, Scott T. Smith. 48, Special Collections and Archives, Merrill Library, Utah State University. 50 (INSET), Scott T. Smith. 50-51, Scott T. Smith. 53, Photograph courtesy of the Forest History Society, Durham, NC. 54-55, Scott T. Smith. 56 (INSET), Courtesy USDA Forest Service/Scott Bushman. 56-57, Phil Schermeister. 59, Scott T. Smith. 60, Scott T. Smith. 63, Library of Congress. 64-65, Courtesy USDA Forest Service. 67, Phil Schermeister. 68, Bruce Dale. 70, Scott T. Smith. 72-73, William Albert Allard, National Geographic Photographer. 74, Used by permission, Utah State Historical Society, all rights reserved. 75, Used by permission, Utah State Historical Society, all rights reserved. 76, Phil Schermeister. 77, Phil Schermeister. 78-79, Scott T. Smith. 80, Phil Schermeister. 82, Phil Schermeister. 84-85, Phil Schermeister. 86, Phil Schermeister. 88, Phil Schermeister. 89, Phil Schermeister. 90-91, Phil Schermeister. 93, Scott T. Smith. 94-95, Scott T. Smith. 96, Phil Schermeister. 98-99, Scott T. Smith. 100, Phil Schermeister. 101, Phil Schermeister. 102, Courtesy USDA Forest Service. 104-105, Phil Schermeister. 106, Phil Schermeister. 108-109, Special Collections and Archives, Merrill Library, Utah State University. 110, Library of Congress. 111 (UP), Special Collections and Archives, Merrill Library, Utah State University. 111 (LO), Special Collections and Archives, Merrill Library, Utah State University. 112-113, Special Collections Dept., J. Willard Marriott Library, University of Utah. 114-115, Scott T. Smith. 116, Phil Schermeister. 118-119, Scott T. Smith. 120, Scott T. Smith. 122-123, Scott T. Smith. 124, Scott T. Smith. 127, Scott T. Smith. 129, Scott T. Smith. 130-131, Scott T. Smith. 132, Michael S. Quinton. 133, Phil Schermeister. 134, Phil Schermeister. 137, Phil Schermeister. 138 (UP), Library of Congress. 138 (LO), Special Collections and Archives, Merrill Library, Utah State University. 140, Phil Schermeister. 143, Phil Schermeister. 144-145, Phil Schermeister. 146, Phil Schermeister. 147 (UP), Library of Congress. 147 (CTR), Special Collections and Archives, Merrill Library, Utah State University. 147 (LO), Special Collections and Archives, Merrill Library, Utah State University. 148 (UP), Special Collections and Archives, Merrill Library, Utah State University. 148 (LO), Phil Schermeister. 150-151, Scott T. Smith. 152, Scott T. Smith. 154, Special Collections and Archives, Merrill Library, Utah State University. 157, The Herald Journal/Mitch Mascaro. 159, The Herald Journal/Mitch Mascaro. 160-161, Special Collections Dept., J. Willard Marriott Library, University of Utah. 163, Scott T. Smith. 164-165, Scott T. Smith. 166, Scott T. Smith. 168-169, Scott T. Smith. 171, Special Collections and Archives, Merrill Library, Utah State University. 172, Special Collections and Archives, Merrill Library, Utah State University. 174-175, Scott T. Smith. 177, Special Collections Dept., J. Willard Marriott Library, University of Utah. 178-179, Phil Schermeister. 180, Phil Schermeister. 181, Phil Schermeister. 182-183, Scott T. Smith. 184, Phil Schermeister. 185 (UP), Joel Sartore. 185 (LO), James P. Blair. 186-187, Scott T. Smith.

LAST UNSPOILED PLACE

By Michael S. Sweeney

Published by the National Geographic Society
John M. Fahey, Jr., President and Chief Executive Officer
Gilbert M. Grosvenor, Chairman of the Board
Nina D. Hoffman, Executive Vice President;
   President, Book Publishing Group

Prepared by the Book Division
Kevin Mulroy, Senior Vice President and Publisher
Leah Bendavid-Val, Director of Photography Publishing
   and Illustrations
Marianne R. Koszorus, Director of Design
Barbara Brownell Grogan, Executive Editor
Elizabeth Newhouse, Director of Travel Publishing
Carl Mehler, Director of Maps

Staff for this Book
Jane Sunderland, Project and Text Editor
Peggy Archambault, Art Director
Dana Chivvis, Illustrations Editor
Marshall Kiker, Illustrations Specialist
Ken DellaPenta, Indexer
Gregory Ugiansky and XNR Productions, Map
   Research and Production
Gary Colbert, Production Director
Lewis Bassford, Production Project Manager
Jennifer A. Thornton, Managing Editor

Manufacturing and Quality Control
Christopher A. Liedel, Chief Financial Officer
Phillip L. Schlosser, Vice President
John T. Dunn, Technical Director
Vincent P. Ryan, Director
Chris Brown, Director
Maryclare Tracy, Manager

Founded in 1888, the National Geographic Society is one of the largest nonprofit scientific and educational organizations in the world. It reaches more than 285 million people worldwide each month through its official journal, NATIONAL GEOGRAPHIC, and its four other magazines; the National Geographic Channel; television documentaries; radio programs; films; books; videos and DVDs; maps; and interactive media. National Geographic has funded more than 8,000 scientific research projects and supports an education program combating geographic illiteracy.

For more information, please call 1-800-NGS LINE (647-5463) or write to the following address:

National Geographic Society
1145 17th Street N.W.
Washington, D.C. 20036-4688 U.S.A.

Visit us online at www.nationalgeographic.com.

Library of Congress Cataloging-in-Publication Data
Sweeney, Michael S.
   Last unspoiled place : Utah's Logan Canyon / by Michael S. Sweeney.
      p. cm.
Includes index.
   ISBN 978-1-4262-0101-1 -- ISBN 978-1-4262-0102-8 ((dlx))
   1. Logan Canyon (Utah)--Description and travel. 2. Logan Canyon (Utah)--Pictorial works. 3. Logan Canyon (Utah) -- History. I. National Geographic Society (U.S.) II. Title
   F832.C3S94 2007
   979.2 ' 12 --dc22

                              20060036713

ISBN 978-1-4262-0101-1
ISBN 978-1-4262-0102-8 (dlx)

Printed in the U.S.A.

Copyright © 2007 National Geographic Society.
All rights reserved. Reproduction of the whole or any part of the contents without permission is prohibited.